COLOR

in

GARDEN DESIGN

COLOR
in
GARDEN
DESIGN

Sandra Austin

The Taunton Press

Taunton
BOOKS & VIDEOS
for fellow enthusiasts

Printed in the United States of America
10 9 8 7 6 5 4 3 2 1

The Taunton Press, 63 South Main Street,
PO Box 5506, Newtown, CT 06470-5506
e-mail: tp@taunton.com

Library of Congress Cataloging-in-Publication Data

Austin, Sandra
    Color in Garden Design / Sandra Austin.
      p.   cm.
    Includes bibliographical references (p.   ) and index.
    ISBN 1-56158-187-9
    1. Color in gardening. 2. Gardens — Design. I. Title.
SB454.3.C64A87   1998   97-13127
635.9'68 — dc21   CIP

ACKNOWLEDGMENTS

This book owes much to the technical skills and enthusiasms of two excellent teachers, Joy Turner Luke and my father, John Attinello, who gave of their time and expertise in color, photography, and design.

I would like to thank Laura Angiolilo, Leigh Baker, Todd Bennett, Francine Cannon, Leigh David, Dianne Holleman, Laurie Lemons, and Liz Lynch of Bailey's epic; LuAnne Cenci of Eastman Kodak; Carolyn Cotton and Anton Hosley of Avanti Case-Hoyt; Kelly Furr of the Optical Society of America; Cathy Hofknecht of Munsell Color; and the design students in George Washington University's Landscape Design program. Thanks also to Barbara Cram, Mary Frogale, Jody Horvath, Louise Hourrington, Pete Luke, Nancy Luria, Rachel Moen, Dick and Joanne Murphy, and Brenda Skarphol, and most of all, to my family.

The fine publishing staff at The Taunton Press were creative, competent, and cheerful guides in bringing this book to publication. Special thanks to Helen Albert, Cherilyn DeVries, Ruth Dobsevage, and Henry Roth.

CONTENTS

INTRODUCTION

Some years ago, I was asked to develop and teach a beginning design course for a university landscape-design program. The students were enthusiastic gardeners with varying degrees of previous design knowledge. Some students had no design background, while others were accomplished artists in other fields, such as painting, graphics, photography, architecture, and interior design. The classes were a fascinating experience, since each student had an individual prejudice about what constitutes good garden design and a design vocabulary that reflected the art form in which he or she had been trained.

My course included a single class about color, but I was often frustrated in efforts to explain color composition in the context of plants and gardens. I realized that paint mixing does not describe what goes on in garden design, but was unaware of any other ordered way to explain color. Landscape architecture books declare the color issue too complex to be dealt with, or just ignore it; gardening books present specific plant combinations that can be quite beautiful but give little generalized information that would help a designer understand when or why certain colors react in a particular way. I had hoped that the Royal Horticultural Colour Charts would offer some practical information for talking about garden color more clearly, but found that without an understanding of how the colors in the charts relate to each other and without a knowledge of why the colors change

appearance so dramatically when the lighting, texture, and surrounding colors change, these charts were little more than a pretty collection of color swatches.

In my search to find a framework to explain color, I came across some books about color in the science, physics, and optics sections of the library that contradicted some of the information I had always read in art and design books, and I was determined to find answers. I read widely but confusedly. There were authors contradicting other authors and theories, and scores of books about color with no color in them— only graphs and mathematical equations. The science books were concerned with observation and measurement, the art books with creative expression, and the garden books with various plant combinations. I spent my time trying to combine the useful attributes of all three, and *Color in Garden Design* is the result.

You may find that what you read in this book contradicts, at least in part, what you have been taught about color relationships. Gardens of great beauty can be created even if artists and designers give inaccurate reasons for using colors in certain ways or combinations. The best way to learn is to observe your surroundings in light of what you read here. Check the sources listed in Further Reading for additional information.

THE BASICS

When you look out at your garden, you see color everywhere, including not only flowers but also leaves, twigs, soil, and the sky. Then the light changes, perhaps the sun goes behind a cloud, and all the colors look different. You may wonder how information about the colors of such different things may be unified, but fortunately, scientists and artists have studied these and other interesting facts about color. They have developed their thoughts and a vocabulary about color in an orderly way that will help you understand what you see around you.

INTRODUCTION TO COLOR

Beginning a book on garden color with photographs of gardens that are famous for their colors is a little like having a music class of beginners, as they sit with their plastic recorders, listen to a Beethoven symphony. It's inspiring and is meant to show the possibilities, but it can also be intimidating.

Great gardens are often overwhelming to beginners because there is so much information to be absorbed. At first, you simply want to enjoy the garden as an artistic composition. At a second glance, you want to understand more about how the garden works—what plants are used and how they grow, what colors are used in what combinations, and how the garden relates to its location. In a basic sense, you want to know why you like it. If you are a designer, you begin to think about garden structure or layout, and such concepts as combinations of texture, form, and, of course, color. To proceed to the next level of understanding, you may study one concept, such as color, in more detail.

To learn about color and to acquire that more detailed knowledge, it helps to have a common language, an agreement that certain words will mean certain things. In art and design, it's not enough to have verbal definitions, but you must have visual examples as well, that is, you must be able to see the colors and understand their relationships. Many people can discuss color verbally, but if you ask them to point to certain colors or color combinations to illustrate a point, there will be a very wide variation in what they choose. It also helps to have visual examples of plants and gardens. In art books on color, you often see paintings or sculptures as examples of certain concepts. These not only acquaint you with different artist's interpretations of a particular idea but also help you to realize that what may seem theoretical actually has a very practical application.

Claude Monet's gardens at Giverny, outside Paris, are famous for their rich palette of colors.

The restored gardens of Celia Thaxter on Appledore Island, one of the Isles of Shoals off the coast of Portsmouth, New Hampshire, offer proof that a small space, simple design, and common plants can have lasting appeal.

Once you have mastered a basic color vocabulary, you can begin to understand why colors react in certain ways when they are in different combinations. Some facts about color composition are fairly evident and easy to understand, but others will make you shake your head in disbelief because they seem to be the exact opposite of what you expect to find. Because each person sees color differently, it is even more important to have visual examples of these effects. Some will seem quite striking and powerful to certain people, but less so to others. It is important that you understand how you yourself see color so that you can look more intelligently at your surroundings and begin to develop your own color compositions.

Knowledge and creativity are not the same thing. Learning about color theory will not necessarily make you a good designer, but it will give you some tools to help you create in something other than a haphazard fashion. Some designs that follow the rules are pleasant but uninspiring; designs that break with traditional rules or combinations may be exciting and attractive. It is a further test of the design to see what happens to it over time. Perhaps the boring and uninspiring will become a favorite garden that people visit over and over again, seeing subtle design relationships that are not immediately evident; perhaps the jarring modern effort will become the first in a new style or school of garden design.

The gardens at Wave Hill in New York represent a grand style of gardening, with sophisticated variations of color schemes using unusual plants.

This emotional connection to the physical design is so difficult to predict and understand that some people say design cannot be taught. Yet the alphabet and sentence structure are taught in elementary schools, in spite of the fact that very few of the students grow up to be creative writers, and even fewer become famous authors. Most of us can communicate verbally at a comfortable level; we can make ourselves understood, express our emotions, and keep our personal affairs in good order. So should it be with design.

Just as you can learn the alphabet and choose to write to your friends, write a sitcom, or write a great novel, you can learn the basic information about color and design a foundation planting for your home, a great perennial border, or a famous display garden. You will also appreciate your surroundings more if you understand the colors you see every day.

Perhaps the most exciting role of more detailed and accurate color knowledge will be in spurring creativity. Many designers will be able to take the information in this book and look at their gardens in a new way, and create gardens that can't yet be imagined. There is a strong need for new design solutions in gardening and landscaping, and color offers one possibility for organizing and discovering these new designs.

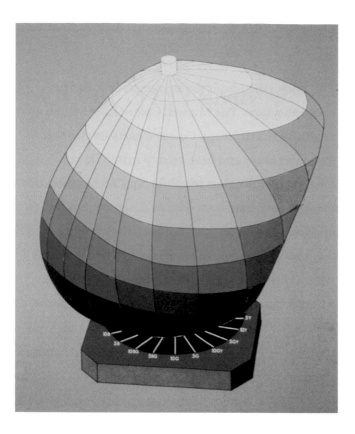

Left: the Munsell color solid. Suppose you had to describe how all the colors in the world relate to each other visually. Albert Munsell imagined a sphere but came to realize that the sphere would have to be irregular to explain variations in human vision. The bulges in the yellow and blue regions are your first clue that describing color perception is a complicated task.

Below: Munsell color charts. Although the color solid is a useful concept, the presentation of colors in books and swatches is a more practical approach.

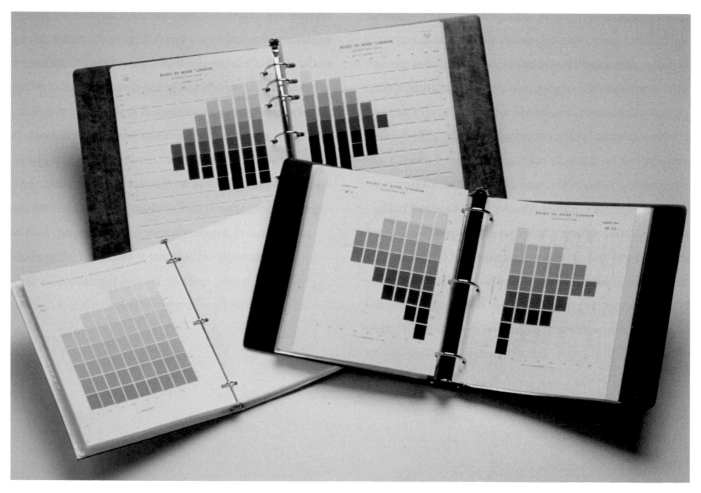

Munsell Color-Order System

The Munsell Color-Order System is an American classifying system that is used as a standard for color notation in artistic, commercial, scientific, and educational work. Developed by an artist, Albert Munsell, for use by artists and designers, it can be used to specify colors and show the relationships among colors. The Munsell system defines a color in terms of three qualities or attributes: hue, value, and chroma. Gradations of color are based on the way people see, not on formulations of paint or other colorant mixing, so that the color of any surface can be identified by comparing it to color chips that are arranged according to steps of visual discrimination.

The Munsell system, acknowledging that color relationships do not fall in equal steps, expresses color relationships as an irregular sphere. The sphere has the pure hues or colors such as red, blue, green, and yellow around its equator. As the colors move toward the core, they become more gray, or decrease in chroma. The vertical axis of the sphere is a neutral gray scale, showing the attribute called value; it progresses from black at the bottom to white at the top. By dividing the sphere into vertical, horizontal, and radial planes, any color can be located in relation to others, and given a numerical reference. Color chips are presented in charts. Each chart is formed from a vertical slice of the sphere, representing a single hue or color and its value and chroma steps—it's a useful presentation for a designer wishing to compare colors.

One difference between the Munsell system and other systems you may know is that Munsell based his system on 10 basic hues so that the finer discriminations between hues could be described with decimals. Most artist's systems are based on six hues; the difference is in the naming and the steps, though the basic colors exist in all systems.

Royal Horticultural Society Colour Charts

The Royal Horticultural Society (RHS) Colour Charts are an English classifying system for flower color. The charts show the three attributes of color: hue, brightness (Munsell's value), and saturation (Munsell's chroma). The charts were derived from the Munsell system; you can match Munsell values to the RHS colors, but they do not appear in the same order. In the RHS system, the colors are arranged by color hues except for the strongly desaturated (grayed) colors. There are four color groups: the yellow to red group, the red to blue group, the blue to green group, and the grayed colors. The grayed colors include the grayed variations of all the hues in the other three groups plus browns, but are not directly related in the system to any particular hue. Color names found in the early versions of the system are no longer used; the colors are classified by letter and number groups.

Royal Horticultural Society Colour Charts.

CIE

In 1931 the Commission Internationale de l'Eclairage (CIE) established an international system for specifying color based on the chromaticity diagram. This roughly horseshoe-shaped diagram, shown on the facing page, represents the theoretical limits of human vision. No color in nature, or color that can be made with pigments, dyes, or phosphors, can ever reach the outside boundary of the diagram. The center of the diagram represents white; the edges are hues representing various wavelengths.

The diagram includes a coordinate system that specifies any color with three numbers. In industry, a color is measured with an instrument that obtains its CIE coordinates, a specification understood throughout the world. The CIE system also defines standard observers and illuminants, which represent how an average person sees color and common sources of light.

Color spacing within the diagram is not visually uniform. However, colors specified with CIE notation can be converted to other systems, including Munsell, RHS, and printing systems. With the intrusion of computers into the art and design world, the ability to understand color specification will become important to even the casual designer.

In the RHS system, the color charts, or swatches, come in the form of color fans with holes cut out of the center of the individual swatch. A plant may be placed directly under the swatch for ease of comparison. The fans are used primarily for color identification by botanists and horticulturists, and are not arranged in equal visual steps within the hue fans. This limits their usefulness to designers interested in color relationships.

PRINTING COLOR

Printing systems are colorant systems based on the quantities and qualities of ink or dyes used in the printing process. Systems are based on combining different colors of inks, such as CYM (cyan, yellow, magenta) or CYMK (cyan, yellow, magenta, black), and are sometimes also called three- or four-color processing, respectively. You may also know these designations if you use some computer design packages. All the colors that you see in a book or magazine result from a combination of three or four colors and are limited by the range of the colorants, the inks or dyes, and the quality of the paper upon which the images are printed. But those are not the only limitations. The colors you see in the photographs in this or any book are also limited to the colors seen by the film of the camera. Most films are designed to make human flesh tones look correct and are also concerned with creating true whites, blacks, and grays, as well as some common colors, such as sky and grass. Some colors, such as yellow-greens, pinks, and oranges, as well as the blues found in nature, are not captured accurately. If the film is corrected for these colors, then often the more common colors appear distorted.

The ultimate result is one that you always suspected; books and photographs cannot completely capture the amazing range of color you see when you're actually in the garden.

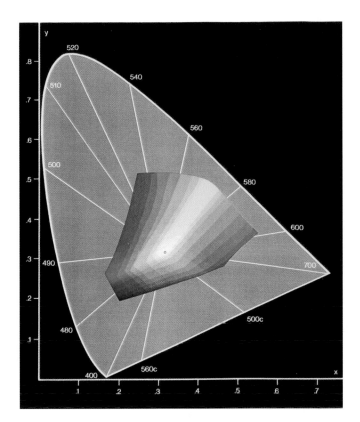

A CIE chromaticity diagram. The horseshoe-shaped outer boundary represents the limits of human color vision; the central area represents the more limited range of colors that printing inks can reproduce.

COLOR NAMES

Color names such as vermilion, verdigris, apricot, and salmon, which are so evocative and pleasurable in writing and speech, can be exasperating when you are trying to be precise about color. If you think the basic color vocabulary of red, green, yellow, and blue is as clear as black and white, you may change your mind as you read this chapter, which deals with the way we describe the colors of the rainbow, as well as white, black, and gray.

CHROMATIC COLORS

When people look at a rainbow, they name the colors red, orange, yellow, green, blue, and violet, as the colors appear from the top of the rainbow. These colors are called chromatic, or spectral, colors, and each color name represents a band of colors that fall within a recognized range. People rarely think about the different colors represented by the name "red" unless they need to match a specific red, such as the red in a rose. It is then that they begin to realize how limiting color names can be.

If you are looking at a representation of the visual spectrum and trying to name the colors you see, you notice some things that may strike you as unusual. When you see the colors arranged in a band (as they are in the spectrum on the facing page), you notice that the color called violet is most physically unlike the color called red; they are, respectively, the shortest and longest wavelengths. Furthermore, you can't even find anything that looks like purple or reddish purple, even though you have always considered it a rainbow color.

Artists care about how colors relate in appearance, so they choose to display color information in a circular form that seems to makes more sense in terms of how color is seen. The spacing in a color circle is regular, rather than uneven, as in the spacing of the chromatic

The Visible Spectrum Meets a Color Wheel

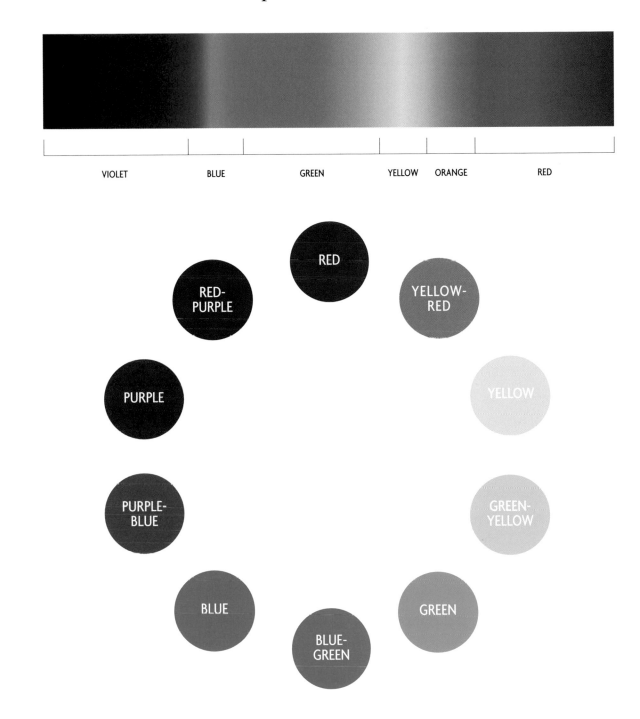

VIOLET　　BLUE　　GREEN　　YELLOW　ORANGE　　RED

The colors of an artist's color wheel do not correspond exactly to the colors of the visible spectrum. The artist joins the two ends of the visible spectrum to form a circle, filling the gap with purplish colors. This produces a useful tool for analyzing color relationships.

bands, so the color names fall in a regular sequence. The reds, purples, and violets that may be different in terms of wavelengths appear similar in human vision, and so the color circle bridges this gap to complete the circle. The color wheel appears to describe a very natural progression of colors.

Because of the confusion in even the simplest of color names, most color systems, including the Munsell and the RHS systems, now describe intermediate colors with number and letter designators, instead of color names. While you may prefer to identify an artemisia as gray-green instead of 7.5GY 5/2, there is a real advantage to having specific color designations when needed.

Gardeners deal not only with common color names, but with botanic names as well. Often botanic names refer to perceived color, using words that may no longer have a popular shared meaning and may include other attributes such as texture (*candicans* implies not only a white color, but a woolly texture) and form (*albomaculatus* means having white spots, *albispinus* means white spined). In a general sense, these names will give you clues about a plant's appearance, such as being more reddish or greenish, but not precise color information.

ACHROMATIC COLORS (WHITE, BLACK, AND GRAY)

White, black, and gray are achromatic (having no hue), or neutral.

Think of white and black in the following ways:

In human vision: They are colors because they arouse sensations.

As light: White is not a color, but the sum of all radiations; black is the total absence of light.

As paint: White is a primary pigment; it cannot be obtained from other colors; black is a secondary pigment because it is mixed using other colors.

White is the lightest color; black is the darkest. But as a practical matter, there are rarely absolute whites or blacks, just as in the garden, there are not true white or black flowers or foliage. When you look closely at white in the garden, you can almost always discern a secondary or underlying color in the eye, bud, or petal of a flower, and with practice (and a glossy piece of white paper for comparison) you can see the color gradation (yellowness, greenness) of the white. Upon close examination, you can almost always identify the true color or colors. This is just as true for black—black flowers and foliage are found upon close examination in clear light to be blues, purples, and greens, darkened nearly to the point where they lose their color identity and are referred to as black.

WHITE AND BLACK

Flowers commonly referred to as black or white rarely are—there is usually an underlying color. For example, the black hollyhock is really a dark red.

GRAY

Few plants are true neutral gray—most, like the ones shown here,
are a pale green or green-yellow.

Other than flowers and foliage, you can talk about seeing white and black in other places in the garden, although it is more accurate to say that you see light and dark colors. Haze and fog cast a whitish film over objects, and the yellowish-white glare of a hot summer's day bleaches out many colors. Snow and ice can have a bluish cast from the reflected light of the sky, or a yellowish-white glare from the sun. Both white and black are common colors for garden furniture and furnishings such as fountains, fences, and lattice work. Black appears to be seen in shadows and shade, again showing a bluish cast from the reflected light of the sky, or some other color from the light reflected by nearby objects. Finally, as evening approaches and light in the garden decreases to the point where the eye can no longer discern colors, you see your surroundings in terms of near-blacks and whites and the gradations in between.

Think of gray in the following ways:

As light: Gray colors are produced by reducing the intensity of white light.

As paint: Very dark gray or gray-black can be achieved by mixing varying amounts of black and white or two complementary pigments (such as violet and yellow).

Grays in the foliage and flower garden are not true grays, but most often pale yellow-greens, such as lamb's ears and artemisia, and pale greens and bluish greens such as some sedums and blue fescue. Certain textural characteristics—small hairs or wax—reflect surface light and cause the graying aspect of these plants. Their color is changed by weather and temperature conditions, often appearing more green or blue in winter, in shade, just before bloom, or when wet. The bark of trees and shrubs is a darker reddish or yellowish gray, such as the reddish gray of flowering cherry. The underlying color becomes apparent only when you hold a true achromatic gray next to the object.

When you look at a distant landscape, you often describe the objects far away as being gray or blue-gray. Pollution can give haze and fog a grayish or yellow-gray cast, which throws a film over all but the closest objects. Grays also describe many weathered objects such as wood, as well as stone colors, which have a wide range of underlying colors from yellows and reds to blues and purples.

COLOR ATTRIBUTES

A color cannot be objectively judged or
measured alone; you can, however, match colors
when seen together under similar conditions,
or compare colors against a standard system. It is
customary to describe colors using three attributes,
or qualities. The first attribute, hue, refers to the
location of the color on the spectrum. The second
attribute, value, refers to the lightness or darkness of the
color; all colors can be lightened or darkened without
losing their essential quality of hue. The third attribute of
a color is saturation, or color content; colors can vary
in saturation from an almost neutral gray to a pure hue.
Once you understand what each of these attributes
means and how to identify it, you can describe any
color that you wish to duplicate. A knowledge of
attributes also helps you in designing to understand
that a color should be lighter, darker, or
grayer to achieve a certain effect.

HUE

*H*ue is the name for the attribute of color that defines its position on the spectrum, such as red, yellow, or green. When people ask "What color is that?" they are almost always talking about the hue, and in common usage, the word "color" is often used when the more precise term "hue" would be more appropriate. For practical purposes, artists often limit the number of hues that they use to discuss color relationships because they can describe most of the important relationships with those basic hues.

Hue is considered to be important because it is the quality of color that carries the emotional content. Symbolism is one expression of this aspect of color, and most us understand the emotional meaning of green when it is said to represent restfulness and nature. As different societies and cultures have become interrelated, symbolism has become more complex, but it is still common to read that red is exciting, green is soothing, blue is cool, and orange is hot. With few

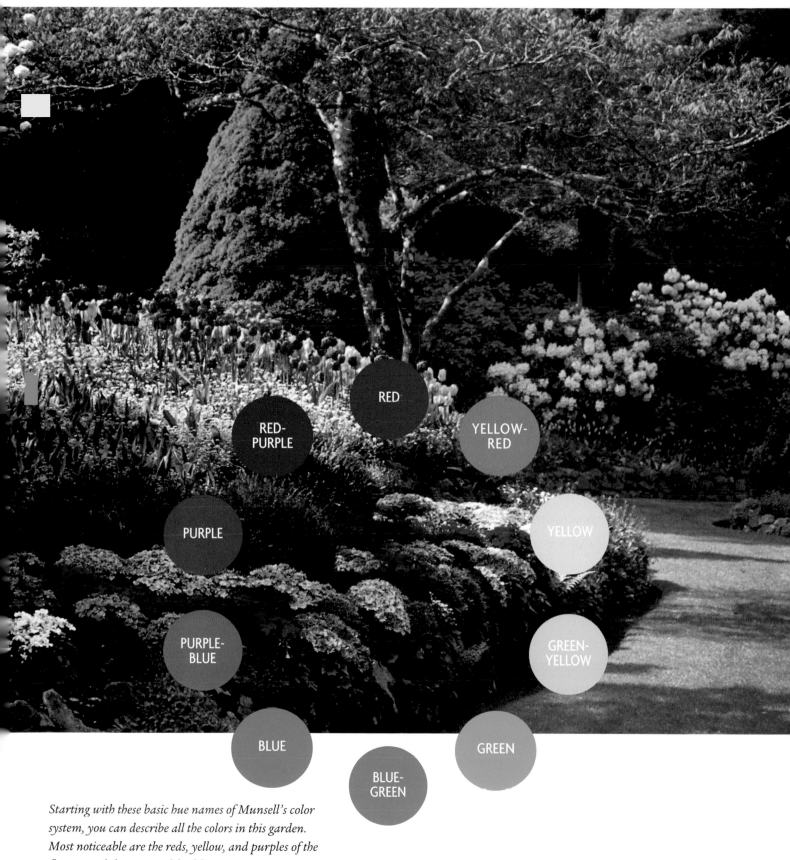

Starting with these basic hue names of Munsell's color system, you can describe all the colors in this garden. Most noticeable are the reds, yellow, and purples of the flowers and the greens of the foliage.

exceptions, these statements about the emotional content of color have not been proven scientifically to have a physical basis (that is, seeing red does not increase your heart rate or raise your blood pressure), but that does not mean that they are not valid or important ideas. It is wise, however, for the designer to remember that the same color can carry different emotional messages depending on its use and context.

When you see color or hue in a garden, you recognize the complexity of its effect. It is unusual for pure hue to occur in the garden or landscape because you are not looking at flat or uniform surfaces. Light plays off of surfaces in a way that makes the object's color seem to change. If you have ever tried to match paint chips or flat color to a flower, you know the complexity of the task, yet, there are similarities enough that you can train your eye to recognize the quality of hue in a flower, and match it to a color chip or swatch.

What affects hue? Hue is a result of light that is absorbed by an object and light that is reflected back from the object. Another way to think of this complex subject is that the object has a color and the reflected light has a color; as both vary, the color you see changes. You know that paint chips with a matte (flat) surface look different from paint chips with a glossy (shiny and smooth) surface. Plants also have matte and glossy surfaces, as well as hairy, glaucous, or patchy surfaces, all of which change the appearance of the color.

Hue is also influenced by the size and shape of the color area; colors look different when they are massed in different size and shape groupings. Perhaps one reason that native plants are not often used in color accent plantings is that the flowers are so small that they don't give the visual impact of a similarly sized planting of large-flowered daylilies, iris, or cannas, or the massed color effect of petunias, impatiens, or salvia. The individual flower color is as bright as the larger flowers, it just occupies a relatively smaller space.

Hue is always influenced by surrounding colors and backgrounds. Lighting (the time of day, time of year, atmospheric conditions, sun, and shade) and the distance of the observer from the color will change the appearance of the hue. Whether the background is dark or light, gray, or pure, hue has a strong effect on the apparent color of any object, flower, foliage, or garden bench. These effects are the basis of many optical illusions and perceptual relationships that intrigue designers in all fields.

PRIMARY AND SECONDARY COLORS

Primary colors are those colors from which all other colors may be derived through mixing. Secondary colors are created when two primary colors are combined. Mixing pigment and mixing light produce different results, and the primary colors for each are also different. The colors are the same; a red will be a red whether it is light or pigment, but it is important to understand that different substances react differently to mixing. When you know what the primary colors are, you will know how to produce the possible range of colors with the minimal number of colors.

The best place to begin a discussion of primary colors is with the colors that are primary colors in human vision. Color receptors, called cones, respond to roughly three bands of visible light, which are called red, green, and blue. Within the eye, it is the response to light that is studied, so when speaking of color, reference is made to light and mixtures of light, rather than paint. Paint is not suited to such color-vision studies because pigment colors reflect multiple wavelengths. Light beams, on the other hand, can be reduced to a narrow band of wavelengths, which allows for more accurate studies.

In mixing light, for work in television and computers as well as theater lighting, the primaries are called additive primaries, because in mixing the colors, lights are added together (think of multiple lights, getting lighter and lighter). Red, green, and blue are the additive primaries. Red and green produce yellow, blue and green produce cyan (a greenish blue), and red and blue produce magenta (a purplish red), the secondary colors of light. When you mix the three additive primaries the result is white, the color of light.

The secondary colors of light are the primary colors of pigment and inks. These subtractive primaries (magenta, cyan, and yellow) are a more accurate way of

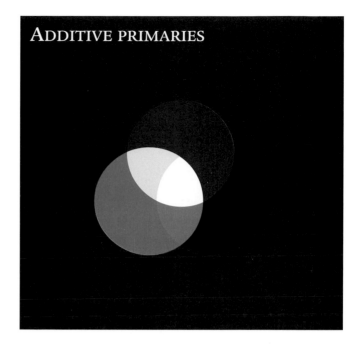

ADDITIVE PRIMARIES

The additive primaries (red, green, and blue) show how light mixes.

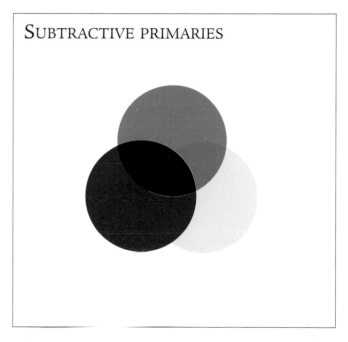

SUBTRACTIVE PRIMARIES

The subtractive primaries (magenta, cyan, and yellow) show how pigments and dyes mix.

UNIQUE HUES IN COLOR VISION

The four "unique" hues in human vision (red, green, blue, and yellow) result from a transformation in the visual system of the three visual primaries.

OPTICAL MIXING

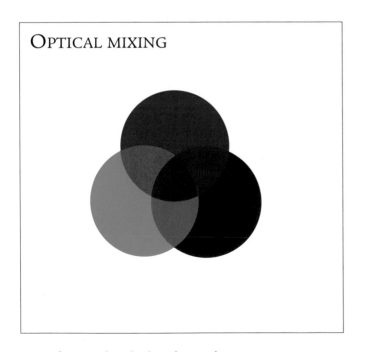

Optical mixing describes how the visual primaries of red, green, and blue combine as you look at objects around you.

describing red, blue, and yellow—the primary colors you know from your school days. Artists in the past were more concerned with precision in mixing paints than in observed color. As production became a part of art (think about book and magazine printing and the impact of computers on the graphic arts), it became necessary to be more precise in color mixing, and so now magenta, cyan, and yellow are the terms used to describe the subtractive primaries.

The subtractive primaries are so called because in mixing the pigments, light is removed, or subtracted, from the mixture (think of layers of paint, getting darker and darker). Mixing magenta and yellow yields red, mixing yellow and cyan yields green, mixing cyan and magenta yields blue. When you mix the three subtractive primaries the result is black or a very dark gray.

Due to a transformation of the three additive primaries within the visual system, four colors seem to be unique in human vision and are sometimes referred to as psychological primaries. They are red, green, blue, and yellow, and when combined with white and black, form the basis of all colors that are seen. ("Unique" in this instance refers to the idea that these colors are not perceived as a mixture of other colors, in the way that you can sense the redness and yellowness in the color orange.) The concept is often difficult for painters, who are accustomed to thinking of green in pigment, not as a unique hue, but as a mixture of blue and yellow.

A last type of mixing, called optical mixing or fusion, is a way of expressing the complex interactions between the eye and the brain as you observe your surroundings. In the 1800s, when scientists realized that paint mixtures were not suitable for studying color mixing, they devised a way to show how colors mix optically by using spinning discs. Colors, placed in sectors on discs that are spun rapidly, are averaged together by the eye to produce, in effect, a new color. Although the wavelengths of colors on spinning discs are added together, the result is different from the additive mixing of light. On a disc mixture, the colors combine to form a new color that is an average of the hue, value, and saturation of the original colors. The Impressionist painters, whose work is often cited in garden design, also offer an example of this type of mixture. In their paintings, small amounts of colors seen from a distance fuse to form new colors.

In optical mixing, the primary colors of red, green, and blue combine to form a middle gray, instead of white for additive primaries and black for subtractive primaries. The secondary colors are a darkened yellow (which appears olive), a dark magenta, and a dark cyan. Each of the secondary colors is of a lightness and saturation that is midway between those of the primary colors. In general, optical mixing produces colors that do not lose their lightness (value) and color content (saturation), as happens in paint mixing. Values (lightness) are averaged instead of increasing, as in light mixing. When you look at these colors on the page of this book, they are not very appealing; however

if you superimpose them over the background colors seen outside, you will be surprised to discover that they are in fact like the colors you see in nature. Of all these systems, it is optical mixing that is of primary importance to gardeners.

Although gardeners are not specifically concerned with additive or subtractive mixing, some knowledge of them is a good preparation for the other interactions between colors that occur as you observe colors in the garden. Furthermore, the more you know, the more you can appreciate the confusing and often contradictory words and ideas used in explaining color that arise from these three different situations: the mixing of light, the mixing of pigment, and the mixing of colors in human vision. Each acts differently, but we use the same color words, and sometimes, through lack of knowledge, we confuse the effects of one system with the effects of one of the others. It is only in observing the three kinds of mixing that you can appreciate what is taking place. A book such as this can tell you what to expect and why, but for understanding (and in many cases, believing), you must experiment with the various mixing processes yourself.

BASIC HUES

Almost everyone, artist or not, has a mental image of some basic colors, usually red, yellow, blue, and green, and almost everyone has heard of a color circle, or color wheel. Using a set of basic hues, the artist can look for relationships between the hues, and propose guidelines for use that can simplify complex combinations.

The basic hues are often organized into a circle even though purple-blue and red-purple are at opposite ends of the visual spectrum (that is, the purple-blue has the shortest wavelengths and the red-purple has the longest), because they seem to us to be very similar in appearance. By placing the colors next to each other on a circle (see p. 13), we acknowledge that visual connection. In the process, certain relationships become apparent. Ideas such as colors opposite each other on the wheel and colors next to each other on the wheel, as well as more complex groupings of colors, all owe their existence to the relationships of hues as seen in a color circle.

With these limits, the more noticeable and logical hue relationships become more apparent. It's easy to see that red and blue-green are opposite each other and red and yellow-red are next to each other on the Munsell color wheel; if you learn the basic information about complementary colors (opposites) and analogous colors (colors next to each other), adding information about other intermediate colors can follow a predictable pattern. If you are searching for the color opposite a red that has yellow in it, you know you will have to look for a green that has more blue in it. This points out one area in which the Munsell system has advantages; its five minor hues are named as hyphenated major names (yellow-red instead of orange), and so it is simpler to remember the relationships between hues.

In the Munsell system, basic hues include the five major hues—red, yellow, green, blue, and purple—and five minor hues—yellow-red, green-yellow, blue-green, purple-blue, and red-purple. These basic hues are the hues that are most pure, or saturated, and they are the ones that are commonly included in the color wheel. The color circle or wheel can be thought of as a horizontal slice out of the Munsell color solid, showing the basic hue relationships. You can take any color, find its place in the Munsell system, and estimate the effects of color mixing according to its relative place in the system—is it a different hue? lighter? darker? grayer? All colors are related to the basic hues in one of these ways, and when you learn the system, you can more easily describe and design with all colors.

BASIC HUES

Red, green, purple, orange, yellow. The simple hue names convey the quality
of color we see and remember in plants.

A green garden is the closest gardeners come to a single-hued, or monochromatic, composition. Look carefully, though, and you'll see not only green, but also green-yellow and browns.

SINGLE HUES

Each one of the hues has colors related to that hue in terms of value (light and dark) and saturation, or chroma (grayness). In the Munsell system, these are presented as separate charts or pages, essentially a vertical slice out of the color solid (see p. 8). The idea of a hue page is similar to the idea of a monochromatic, or single-hued, color grouping: one hue with its light, dark, and gray variations.

Monochromatic plantings, unlike monochromatic paintings, photographs or textiles, are nearly impossible, because more than one hue is invariably involved: flowers have foliage, eyes, and other parts that are different hues, and whether or not you are aware of them, they change the way the planting looks. You often read about monochromatic plantings in gardening books; generally the authors are referring to a grouping of flower colors that are related to a given basic hue—a red garden, a yellow garden, or even a white garden. The type of garden that possibly could be limited to one hue family could be a green garden. In most cases, the greens run the range of hues from the green-yellows to the blue-greens, so once again, the planting may not be strictly monochromatic. You can understand the merit of using hue families as an organizing principle, but recognize that in gardening, other plant colors, as well as soil, hardscape, and light colors, interfere with the purity of a single hue composition. For most gardeners, this lack of purity adds interest. Though there are many situations in the arts where true monochromatic compositions are possible and even welcome, gardening doesn't seem to be one of them.

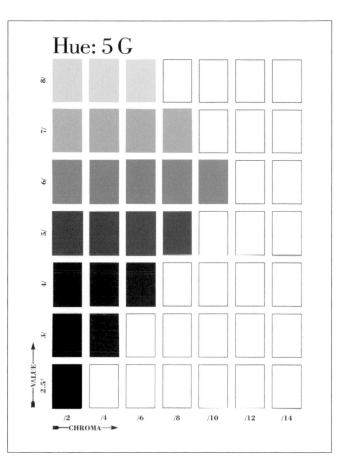

A page from the Munsell Student Color Charts shows the light, dark, grayed, and pure colors that share a green hue.

Single hues are useful as a tool for thinking about color relationships that may not otherwise be apparent. In the red, yellow-red and yellow Munsell hue pages, you see darker, grayed colors (called browns) and lighter, grayed colors (called tan, buff, and light brown), which if not seen with their pure hues, do not seem related. In the red hue pages, you find lighter colors (called pinks) that seem very different from their pure hues. Some of these relationships are very subtle. Only by seeing the range of colors next to each other do you begin to understand the visual connection.

Intermediate Hues

Everyone realizes that there are colors beyond the basic hues, and most people can distinguish between a wide range of separate hues. You may be familiar with intermediate colors through their names given by painters: such colors are referred to as tertiaries, quaternaries, and quinaries, indicating that they are created by mixing primary and secondary pigments in varying proportions. If you were to insert such colors into a color wheel, they would fall between their primary or "parent" colors (the colors mixed to achieve a new color), so that you could locate them relative to the basic hues. This gives you a hint about why intermediate hues are important. They are more complex, which means that in color combinations they can be more influenced by other colors than the basic hues are. For example, a color that has blue and green in it may look more blue or more green, depending upon its surrounding colors. All colors change appearance depending upon the surrounding colors, but if everything else is equal, intermediate colors are more influenced by their surroundings than their surroundings are influenced by them.

Naming intermediate colors presents a thorny problem for designers and gardeners alike. Remember that people can recognize thousands of colors; color systems simply refer to a limited group of distinguishable colors. If you can accept this restriction, you will find that such designations are more than sufficient for general color recognition.

In addition to the intermediate hues, their light, dark, and gray variations abound in the garden. Many of the colors called green in the garden are in fact green-yellows that are of medium lightness and somewhat grayed. Gold in flowers is usually a strong yellow of medium lightness with some red; gold in foliage is more often a green-yellow of medium lightness. Purple is a pure hue in the Munsell system, but as used in the garden can describe a number of intermediate colors. In flower color, the purples that have some blue content are often called blue, such as blue ageratums, blue lobelias, and blue petunias. The purples that have some red content may be called pink if they are light, such as crepe myrtles; if they are medium or dark in value, such as some geraniums, they may be called mauve or magenta. The purples in foliage vary from the very dark purple sedums to the more red-purples found in the fall foliage of the dogwood.

INTERMEDIATE HUES

Not quite red, not quite purple, not quite yellow. When you think of the circle relationships, you can see that the yellow of the tulips is more red and the yellow of the spirea foliage is more green. The purple of the sedum has some red in it; the red of the mums has some yellow.

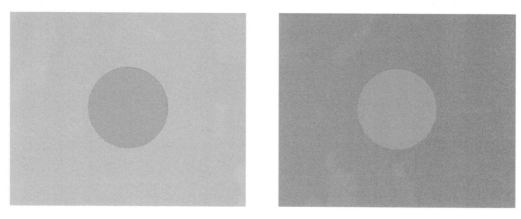

The hue of the bridge shows strikingly against the hue of the foliage. When the same hue is placed against a color that is closer on the color circle, the result is very different.

HUE CONTRAST

Contrast is the perception of differences between two or more effects. It is important in design because it affects unity and balance in a composition, whether the composition is a painting or a garden view. High contrast usually means opposites such as black and white, while low contrast implies similarity, such as shades of gray. High levels of contrast are often exciting and draw the eye, but too much contrast can be considered garish, busy, and distracting. Low levels of contrast can be soothing and restful, but too little contrast can be boring and dull. Finding the appropriate level of contrast is one of the important problems to be solved by the designer.

In much garden writing about color, when the term "contrast" is used, it is contrast of hue that is meant—that is, contrast of the basic colors such as red and green or blue and yellow. Sometimes the other attributes of color are mixed up into the discussion—a light red is contrasted with a dark green, or a grayed green is contrasted with a brilliant magenta. It is, however, possible to discuss contrast of hue separately from contrast of value and saturation, which allows the designer to be more specific about the goals of the garden design.

Generally, high hue contrast means colors that are opposite or nearly opposite each other on a color wheel, and low hue contrast means colors that are next to or near each other on the color wheel. Hue contrast lessens when colors share hues, such as red with yellow-red and red-purple, or green with blue-green and green-yellow. Low hue contrast is often implied in single-color flower gardens whose appeal may be in part due to their unifying effect—when flower color is kept nearly constant, other elements, such as foliage and bark, may not be noticed; attention is focused on the dominant hue. These gardens can be eye-catching; from a distance the individual flower colors will combine to read as a large mass of color. Closer examination reveals a rich tapestry of individual colors in a combination that can be observed and examined without some of the more visually disturbing or tiring effects that hue contrast can create for the eye.

High hue contrast is associated with display gardens, since opposing colors are thought to attract people's attention. Gardens with these contrasting colors may also be considered informal and unsophisticated, such as a wildflower meadow or children's garden, where pure hues of contrasting value are considered desirable. High hue contrast can also exist at different values and saturations, for example, with reds and greens that are light or dark or somewhat grayed. Holding value or saturation constant may lessen the impact of high hue contrast.

VALUE

*T*he second attribute of color is value, sometimes called brightness, lightness, or luminosity. Value describes the light or dark quality of a color, which is determined by the amount of light reflected back from an object. White reflects almost all light, so it has the highest value and is lightest; black reflects almost no light, and therefore has the lowest value and is darkest.

One tool that artists use to compare values is called a gray scale, a spectrum of grays that show equal visual steps of lightness and darkness, from black at the bottom to white at the top. Because the steps are based on visual differences, the middle gray does not reflect 50% of the light, but only about 19% of the light. The fourth circle from the left is closest to this visual middle gray; the third and

All colors can be measured in value (lightness) by comparing them to a gray scale, which shows the steps of neutral gray from black to white. Notice where the gray circles fade into the photo and where they stand out; you can estimate the values of any part of the foliage and flowers of the astilbe by this simple comparison.

A tree that is in sun and shade seems to be different colors. A more accurate way to describe this dramatic composition is in terms of different values of green and gray.

fourth circles from the right are closest to a 50% light reflectance. Notice how different they seem. This is yet another instance when what you see does not match what you measure. People are more sensitive to small value differences between dark colors than between light colors.

As a practical matter, you can estimate the value or lightness of any color using just the gray scale, instead of using a full set of color chips. Colors with the same value reflect the same amount of light, although not all of the basic hues are the same value (see pp. 38-40).

Each hue also has many values, such as light and dark yellows. Because each hue begins with a different value, the light and dark ranges are different for each hue.

For example, yellow, a very light hue, can be lightened only a little before it seems white. Purple, a very dark hue, can be darkened only a little before it seems black.

A gardener does not change the value of a color as painters do, but may rely on changes that affect the appearance of value, so that colors look lighter or darker. What are these other effects? In an objective sense, value as measured by a light meter is changed when the source, direction, and distance of light are changed. The simplest example in a garden is an object that is in shade and light at the same time. The part in the sun appears to be a lighter color than the part in the shade. The difference is actually one of value, not color.

In a more subjective sense, value is also affected by surrounding objects. The contrasts between colors and value changes according to the eye's ability to adapt to different light and read the differences. You face this aspect of value very often, because it is the contrast of light and dark between the printed word and background of a page that enables you to read the forms that create letters and words. If the value differences are not appropriate (think of blue type on a green background), reading becomes uncomfortable and difficult. The value difference may be in the actual dark and light relation of the print to the page, or may be affected by dim light or the glare of the sun.

Most of the information carried in a picture or scene is conveyed by the contrast of value. This includes the definition of form and the amount and duration of light. Without value contrast, you might not see anything at all—just imagine the absurdity of a picture of a black cat at night eating licorice!

The utility of value contrasts goes beyond simple object recognition. The patterns and arrangement of light and dark are always an important part of any composition, including gardens. Many garden designers affirm that it is easier to lay out the structure of a garden in winter, when the color of flowers and foliage do not distract from the importance of good strong organization. A well-designed garden will stand up to being photographed in black and white, conveying the feeling of beauty simply through the composition of lights and darks.

Winter is a good time to focus on value contrasts and see the composition of a garden without the distraction of bright colors.

Pure yellow will always be a lighter color than pure green.

RELATIVE VALUE OF HUES

All of the basic hues are not equal in value at their maximum color content. The ranking of the hues by value from the brightest (yellow) to the darkest (purple) is sometimes referred to as a natural order of colors. Although most people can rank grays of various values from light to dark with ease, it is more difficult to think of the hues as having different values except in the more extreme cases. Many people will be able to sense that a yellow flower is lighter than its green foliage, but become less sure of the light and dark relationships when trying to relate the value of red to green.

In the Munsell system, for example, yellow has the highest value, followed next by red, green, blue, and purple, which is the darkest of the hues. If colors have the same value, they reflect the same amount of light, no matter what hue. The Munsell notation for value in most cases shows numbers running from 1 (dark) to 9 (light). Absolute black, if it existed, would be 0, and absolute white, if it existed, would be 10. Using these numbers, you can get an idea of the relative value of the basic hues: yellow 9, green-yellow 7, yellow-red 7, green 6, blue-green 5, blue 4, red 4, purple-blue 3, red-purple 3, purple 2.

These numbers have been used in an interesting system of balancing colors, an idea that was at one time considered important to designers. Because of their

The Natural Value of Hues

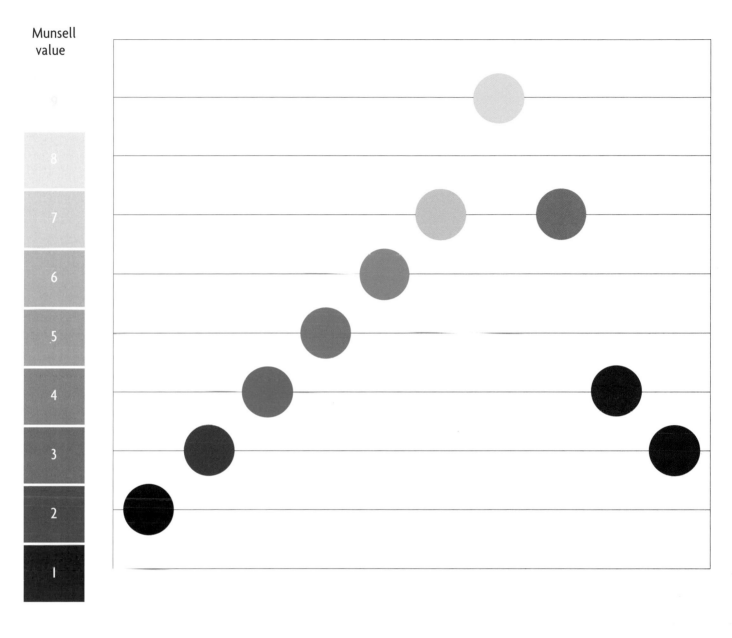

Munsell value

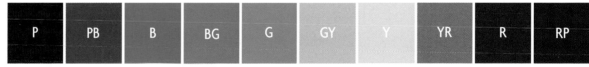

Munsell hue

The basic hues each have a different value, ranging from purple, the darkest, to yellow, the lightest.

very different lightness, yellow and purple in equal amounts are said not to balance. If you want them to appear balanced in combination, you have two choices. You can darken the yellow and lighten the purple until they are closer in value, or you can change the relative amounts of each color. If you are combining the pure hues, you will need roughly three to four times the amount of purple to balance an equal amount of yellow. All colors can be visually balanced in this way. In general, this system of balancing colors through value suggests that more of a darker color is needed to balance a lighter color, if both colors are at maximum saturation.

A balanced relationship between colors doesn't guarantee a beautiful composition, but it does help you understand how one aspect of a color—value—can be used to create color combinations. A composition that is completely balanced may seem very dull; a scene that is wildly out of balance may be very exciting.

In addition to the complication of different hues having different values, lighting changes the value ranges for each hue. The reds, oranges, and yellows look darker in lower light, such as shade or twilight, and the blues and greens look lighter.

HIGH VALUE

Tints are the name painters have given to light colors, the colors that have high values or reflectance. The name comes from the process of lightening paint colors, where paints with white pigment added to them are referred to as tints. If only value is increased, there should not be a shift in hue or saturation, but the term is often more loosely used to indicate any light color. In the Munsell system, colors of high value are all the colors in the top half of the color solid, or the top half of each of the color charts.

Because colors with high value have greater reflectance, they may be more visible and noticeable than even the pure hues. It is often the case that light colors will appear to advance toward the observer when the background is darker and/or grayer, and may often appear to be larger than their darker counterparts. Light colors often also give the appearance of more openness and space; in interior design a light room is considered more open and larger, a darker room more closed and smaller.

In gardens, the equivalent of interior walls may be dark hedges and tall plantings, or fences, and the "ceiling" is usually the light of the sky or the dark canopy of foliage overhead. These structural elements of the garden or garden room are rarely the focus of attention, but their lightness and darkness can be changed to alter the openness of the garden. Just as a room can have one wall painted a different color,

All hues have a range of dark and light values. The different purples in the cineraria flowers give you an idea of the range of values within a single hue, enhanced by the shading and lighting over the surfaces of the blossoms.

garden rooms can have hedges and fences that differ in color and lightness. Designers wishing to open up a garden space or make it appear taller can choose trees with a light canopy, such as a honeylocust, trim tree limbs up higher so that more light can come in, or in the case of pergolas and other overhead garden structures, keep the paint colors lighter.

Light colors show up best on a dark background. The darker garden greens can highlight the light colors, and make them glow, especially if they are in shade or part shade, or seen at twilight. You have probably read of white or pastel gardens in particular that have these qualities. Light colors can get lost in strong sunlight, especially if in a situation like an urban garden, they are surrounded by the very high-valued, highly reflective surfaces, such as concrete, marble, and light stone, and if they have a low level of saturation, or color content. When light reflectance from the sun and sky is so high, there may be an uncomfortable feeling of glare and heat. One way to minimize this effect is to increase the amount of green in the plantings. The traditional garden solution is to place clipped low-growing green shrubs as borders, or the more naturalistic greens of low grasses and foliage plants, perhaps not arranged in a straight line, but in curves or drifts.

Low Value

Colors that are darkened have lower values and are sometimes referred to as shades (the term comes from painting, where adding black pigment to a hue gives a lower value). Some of the darker hues, such as the blues and purples, are, at their pure level, so low in value already that only a little darkening can take place before the hue becomes unrecognizable. Shading may also describe the darkening and graying of a color. On a Munsell chart, when a hue is simply darkened, its darker hues are directly below it (see p. 29); when the hue is darkened and grayed, its darker hues run in a diagonal line from the outside of the solid toward the central column. Most pure hues can be darkened only one or two steps before they become grayed. This is similar to what you see in nature; shadows and shade appear not only darker, but also grayer.

In the garden, dark colors tend not to be seen very well against a dark-green background, especially when seen from a distance. In contrast, a lighter background of concrete and buildings makes dark colors show up quite well, particularly if the color content is high, such as a magenta or purple.

Another interesting group of low-value colors is in the shaded part of the garden, or the shadows. Shadows and shade are caused by the sunlight being blocked, usually by trees or buildings. Shaded areas and shadows appear much darker when they are surrounded by areas in full sunlight. Areas in sun look much lighter, and sometimes even washed out, when seen from a shaded point of view.

Flowers that appear to be red in a garden setting are often the darker shades. As you can see, when red is lightened, it may look more orange than is expected.

The first thing you notice in this photo is probably the common white impatiens. Its mass of light-colored flowers is set off by the darker and grayer background of foliage and stone.

Value Contrast

Scenes that have a high contrast of value, or many lights and darks, will be dramatic and eye-catching. However, value contrast that is too extreme may be the underlying cause of what is commonly called a "busy" composition, a picture in which the eye moves nervously back and forth between elements, trying to find a point of interest. In a garden, you have the light and dark colors of the flowers and foliage, but also the light and dark spots of open and planted areas, and the lights and darks of sun and shadow, with many intermediate steps in between. You have probably been in gardens where extreme contrast of light and dark has made your eyes very tired or where low levels of value contrast made it difficult to discriminate between objects.

Value is an aspect of garden design that differs from planting design. The garden designer must understand how people see as they move through a garden, and realize that the lighting conditions, which may change from day to day and season to season, may be quite important in the enjoyment of the planting designs. As a person moves from shade to sun, the eye adapts fairly quickly, but if the light difference is too great, the strong glare may result in physical discomfort. Moving into dense shade after standing in full sun requires a little more adaptation time from the eyes. Although it is not painful, it usually takes longer than the shade-to-sun adaptation, and during that period, the person may not be able to see clearly, so that uneven paving or rough ground may be more hazardous. An

intermediate or transitional zone, where the value differences are not so great, can help the eye adapt more comfortably as the person moves through the garden. This not only relieves the visual discomfort, but also allows the colors of the entire garden to be seen. When there is too much light, colors are washed out and yellowish; when there is too little light, colors cannot be recognized by the eye.

Value contrast is also important in the composition of flower beds and garden accents, including paving and the various types of garden ornaments. Objects that are lighter, or higher in value, will seem closer, particularly if the background is dark. If you want to highlight an object, make the surrounding plantings darker. If, however, you wish the objects to be part of the garden and not the focus of attention, include flowers and foliage that are similar in value. A birdbath of light stone, or flowers that are white, will be more visible in a garden of dark-green foliage than in a gray garden. Similarly, paths and paved areas can be highlighted or merged into the garden setting, depending upon whether they are made of materials that are lighter or darker than their surroundings, or similar in value.

SATURATION

Saturation is the third attribute of color. It is also called intensity, purity, brilliance, or in the Munsell terminology, chroma. Saturation is a measure of the color content or the strength of a color. Pure hues are the most saturated of colors, and grays are the least saturated. Saturation may be the most difficult of the attributes to understand because the definition of saturation changes with the medium.

In gardening and in observed color, a color that has low saturation (often called desaturated or unsaturated) is one in which grayness is seen. Some examples are the colors of brick, which is an orange or red that has low saturation and medium value (grayed, and somewhat darkened); the browns of mulch, which is also orange with low saturation and low value; and the gray foliage plants, such as the artemisias, which are a green of low saturation and high value (grayed and lightened). Very often, gardeners think of these colors as more natural than their more highly saturated hues.

A mass of brightly colored impatiens catches your eye before the background wall, which is of a similar hue but less saturated.

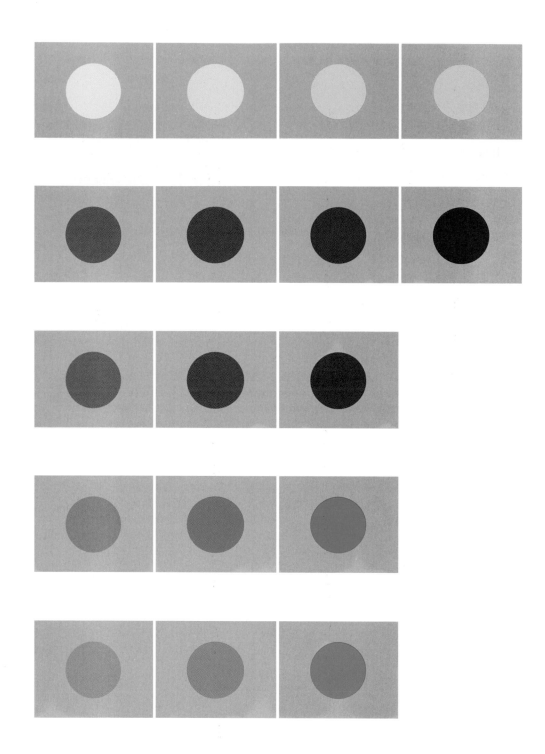

The number of steps of saturation depends on the hue and value. Yellow and red are colors of higher saturation than purple, blue, and green; that is, there are more equal steps between the grayed color and the pure hue.

In other arts, saturation often has a very different meaning. In the print and photographic world, low saturation means a picture that looks washed out, usually with very light or pale colors. Colors that are highly saturated are those that are very intense. In painting, a pure color can lose its high level of saturation by being mixed with white, black, or gray, as well as with other hues, in such a way as to lessen its color content.

The term "saturation" can be thought of as in science: A solution is said to be saturated when a liquid cannot absorb more of a substance. In color, if you started with gray and added red little by little until you reached the pure hue of red, you would understand the steps of saturation of a color as it goes from an unsaturated red (mostly gray, little red) to a saturated red (mostly red, little gray)—the point where the mixture can absorb no more color. This is how Munsell used the term "chroma," and the reason becomes apparent when you consider the achromatic colors: white, black, and gray (see p. 14). A highly saturated black (think of as pure a black as you can imagine) has no chroma; the same holds true for gray and white. You can see how confusion arises. Since it is unusual for the achromatic colors to exist in the garden, saturation, a term with which more gardeners are familiar, means the relative amount of gray or pure hue in a color.

Saturated colors add zing to the garden. A bed of flowers with colors that are highly saturated will stand out and grab the attention of passersby, particularly if the surrounding colors (plants, soil, mulch, buildings) are less saturated. This is probably why so many bedding schemes are formulated from highly saturated hues such as red and yellow—they want your attention.

Surrounding colors have a strong influence on saturation, as do distance and illumination. In a garden, where the variation and complexity of the surrounding colors can be great, a color can look different as a person moves through. A saturated flower may seem incredibly bright and pure against the background of wood or stone, but when seen against or with other highly saturated flowers, its brightness will seem not so intense.

Distance tends to gray colors, and the type and position of the light source will affect the appearance of saturation. In paint and print media, distance is not usually so great that this issue surfaces, but in gardening and landscape design, it's a major factor.

When the light source is either too strong or too weak, the saturation of the color is weakened. You know when you visit a garden in the glare of midday sun that colors tend to appear washed out, and in the low light levels of dusk and dawn, it is always difficult to see pure color.

You can appreciate the saturated color of the small scarlet gilia when you are close to it.

FULL SATURATION

You see colors in the garden at their fullest saturation when you can get close to them and when you can block out some of the effects of competing colors in your field of vision. You probably know this if you read garden picture books; some of the most spectacular photographs are close-ups of flowers and foliage, where everything else has been cropped out or blurred out of focus. This gives you a hint for making colors look intense in the garden: Allow people to be in a position to see the colors without distraction. For

smaller-flowered plants, this means closer. Flowers that droop down should be above the observer—for example, hellebore on a hillside or fuchsia in a hanging basket. Flowers that face upward should be below the observer.

Hues that are at their full saturation, such as the basic hues, appear to be closer than their grayed counterparts. This is easy to remember as it is often seen in the landscape; grayed blue or grayed green mountains recede in the distance when more saturated colors are nearby. The concept applies to lesser

The saturated color of the small yellow honeysuckle flower can be enjoyed even from a middle distance when it is repeated in a mass such as this. When seen up close, further color details and individual blossoms can be distinguished.

distances as well, though the dimensional effect is not as strong. Placing the more saturated colors nearer to the observer may create a feeling of depth in the garden, particularly if grayer or darker colors are in the background. Saturated colors appear to have a hard edge, a characteristic associated with objects that are nearby. If saturated colors are placed in the background, the effect is to "flatten the space," i.e., make things in the distance appear closer. Gardens that cover a lot of space may use this illusion to draw people to a far spot or a location somewhat off the usual path; someone catching a glimpse of a strong or vivid color feels encouraged to go to view the object more closely.

Saturated flower colors are often seen in entrance plantings and in theme parks and other public places where maximum attention is wanted. The saturated hues of reds, oranges, and yellows, as well as their lighter and darker hues, such as peach, pink, and gold, are most readily visible in daylight if they can be seen clearly against the background. The saturated hues of purples and blues, when they are of a light value, can also attract attention, even among the foliage greens. When they are dark, they need a lighter background, particularly if they will be seen from a distance.

GRAYS AND BROWNS

Many colors in the landscape are grayed colors. Even grass and foliage, which you may see described as "brilliant" or "vivid," are actually greens that are medium or low in both value and saturation; it is the play of light reflection and the surrounding colors that makes us imagine that they are brighter and more colorful than they are. Bark, soils, and stone, which in nature are even less saturated, are seen as grays and browns. These grayed colors are not achromatic grays, as you can easily tell if you hold a neutral gray card next to a tree. Grays and browns in nature are quite subtle and have underlying hues that are sensed but not always recognized, overpowered as they are by their more saturated counterparts in the flower and foliage world. A garden designer can emphasize or contrast those underlying hues to create a subtle sense of three-dimensional unity.

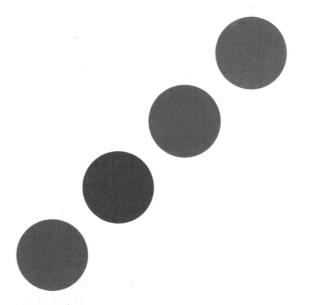

Grayed yellows, reds, blues, and greens appear throughout the garden, although they are rarely the first to be noticed. Learning the underlying hues will help you develop your garden design.

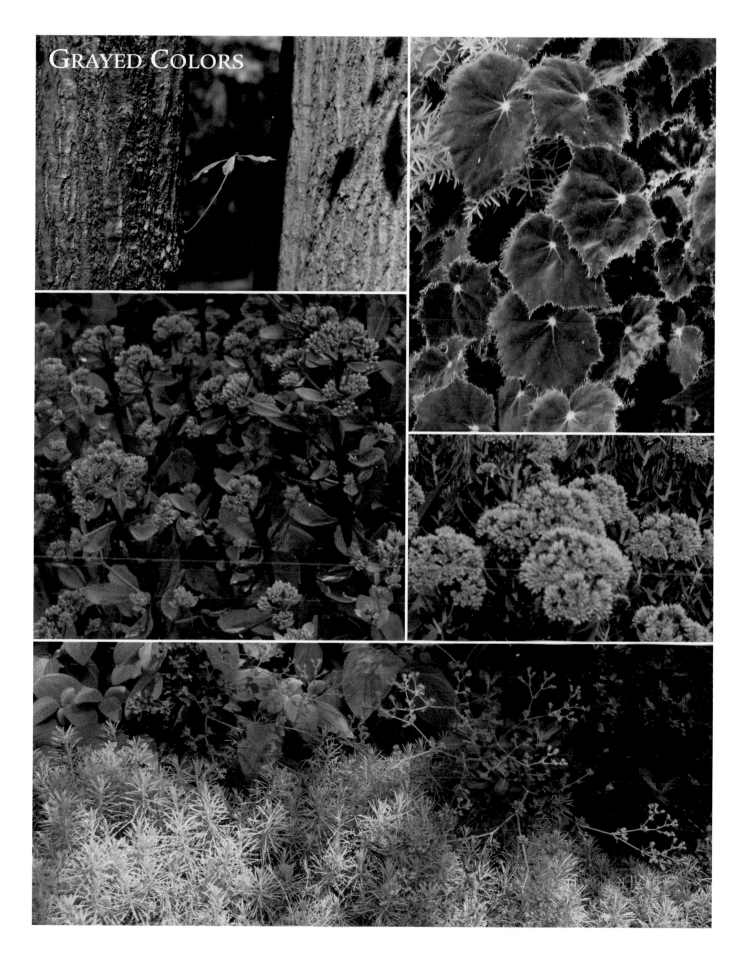

GRAYED COLORS

BROWNS

Browns in nature can range from the light colors of the dried hydrangeas
and ornamental grasses to the deeper browns of bark and soil.

Among the most interesting grayed colors are the browns, or earth colors, which in painting result from the combination of two secondary pigments. Brown is not a hue name, so you don't find any brown in a hue circle, but it is a color name in common usage, and it represents a specific area in the Munsell color solid. It is easiest to understand the browns if you see them in their natural color sequence.

To do that, look at the Munsell color chart below right, where you find browns on the hue page of yellow-red. As you look at the page, you can follow the graying and darkening sequence, showing you that brown is a darker (lower value) and grayer (less saturated) yellow-red. Brown is rarely recognized as a color in its own right because its appearance changes as it darkens. Brown is one case where a different word is used to describe the dark values of a color. Other colors, such as blue, green, and purple, don't have a separate word—we just call them dark blue, dark green, or dark purple.

The grayed yellows, oranges, and reds when they are light or high in value also may not be recognized as related to their hues. Names for these colors include beige, tan, and buff. You may find it so difficult to associate these grayed colors with a particular hue that you will prefer the artistic convention of referring to grays as warm grays (grays with underlying colors of yellow, orange, and red) and cool grays (grays with underlying colors of blue, purple, and green).

All colors appear to gray in the distance. The air between you and distant objects (especially if it is polluted or dusty) is filled with tiny particles that distort light, interfering with your perception of color. Artists know that graying their paint colors makes objects look farther away, giving the illusion of distance. Similarly, in the garden, putting grayed colors in the back of a border and saturated colors in the foreground increases the apparent depth. Reversing the relationship flattens the space. If your garden is seen from more than one viewing point, you will have to be a little more sophisticated about using saturation, or any other aspect of color/distance manipulation.

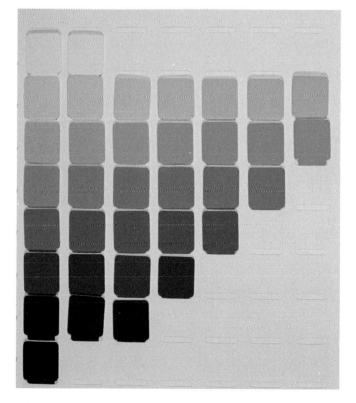

This page from the Munsell Color Charts shows the colors that share the hue yellow-red. Notice the browns and beiges; they are yellow-red hues of different values and saturations.

Colors also appear gray at low light levels. In the early morning and late at night, as well as in very deep shade, colors appear less saturated. You can adjust the amount of light reaching colors with garden lighting (which may distort colors) or by increasing the amount of reflected or direct light. Reflected light may be increased by placing lighter surfaces near where color needs to be seen; direct light may be increased by thinning the shade canopy.

SATURATION CONTRAST

Contrast of saturation refers to the contrast of grayed colors with colors that have a high color content. High saturation contrast occurs when grayed colors are used with saturated colors; low saturation contrast occurs when most of the colors in the garden are either grayed or pure.

High saturation contrast occurs often in flower gardening where grayed foliage and bark are an excellent foil for the striking impact of intensely colored flowers. The backgrounds that are often found in gardens include the grayed and darker greens of hedges, the grayed and darker oranges and reds of brick and wood in buildings and fences, and the warm and cool grays of stone. These colors can become background and not compete with pure hues for attention. In flower gardens where there is too little saturation contrast, the garden may be perceived as being boring (all grayed colors) or fatiguing (the saturated colors of some common classic bedding schemes). Skilled garden designers search for ways to manipulate levels of saturation contrast to create a mood that's somewhere in between. By setting a rhythm of lower and higher saturated colors, you can ensure that attention will be focused where you intend it.

An interesting variation of this design problem occurs in some modern settings, where the houses, latticework, sculptures, or signs are more often painted or colored at fuller saturation. Commercial landscape work often deals with buildings and signs that are in bright, eye-catching colors, and are intended to be the focus of attention. Flower plantings in these instances require a good knowledge of color relationships. The plantings will be of saturated colors that work well with the structure or of grayed colors that will allow the structure to be the primary focus. In such instances, lighting and distance will affect how the colors are perceived; it is not like planting in your backyard.

A subtle study in hue, value, and saturation. The hue of the foliage varies from the yellowish-green of the new growth to the more bluish-green of shaded areas. The gray of the stone has a warm feeling, perhaps having some red and yellow in it. The value contrasts vary from the bright areas to deep shade. The very grayed color of the stone makes the green foliage, a color of middle saturation, seem quite colorful.

COLOR
COMBINATIONS

Combining colors is the point at which many garden design books begin and end. What goes well with pink roses? Should white azaleas be placed next to purple rhododendrons? Thinking of questions such as these, designers have searched for ways to combine plants and other garden elements. In that search, certain relationships between colors emerged and groupings of like colors suggested themselves. Knowing something of hue, value, and saturation, you can reexamine some of these traditional color groupings and understand the underlying relationships.

In the search for unusual color combinations, a garden designer may
look for a subtle color relationship between flowers and foliage. Here
the muted colors of the native Joe Pye weed flowers and the blooms and
foliage of exotic cannas form an unexpected composition.

READING BETWEEN THE LINES

There are many groups of colors that are interesting to artists. Most gardeners have a general idea of words such as pastel, pale, vivid, rich, and muted as they apply to color, but the precise meaning of these words may not be so clear. Defining these words in terms of hue, value, and saturation can help you think more clearly about a color; then you will know better how to use it in the garden.

PASTEL COLORS

Pastel colors have a high value and comparatively high saturation. This means they are light and bright; they reflect a great deal of light and draw the eye. Some pastel color names are pink, peach, primrose yellow, and lavender. When these colors are used in a garden setting where there are lots of foliage greens for background, the effect can be dazzling, particularly in part or full shade. The value contrast between the bright pastels and the greens of the garden creates interesting compositions of light and dark. Pastel colors have enough color content so that you can recognize the hue, so hue combinations are important. It is certainly possible to have a theme of all pastel flower colors, as well as staying within hue families such as light reds (which are called pink) or light yellow-reds (which are called peach).

Plants and flowers that have color variegations or two colors may give the appearance of pastels at certain distances. Leaves with white or yellow variegations may be seen as a lighter green in the distance, and flowers such as daffodils, which may have a strongly yellow or orange-colored cup with white petals, will appear to be a pastel yellow or peach color when seen at a distance. This tendency

of colors to merge into a pastel when seen from a distance offers a great deal of opportunity for the garden designer to create interesting optical effects as the garden is seen by people moving through it or passing by.

Pastels can appear washed out in bright sun, particularly if the background colors are not rich or deep colors. Gardeners faced with light-colored surroundings (concrete, light stone) and high levels of reflectance and glare may find that pastel colors may disappear in such surroundings and look insignificant unless green foliage or darker colors are included, particularly around the edges of the beds.

High in value, high in saturation, the pastel version of the Munsell hue circle reminds you that the basic hue relationships still hold. Most people will recognize the underlying hue of the flowers on the facing page, such as the purple-blue of the agapanthus and the yellow of the rose.

PASTEL COLORS

PALE COLORS

Pale colors have high value and low saturation. Like many flowers, these tulips, moon carrot flowers, and hydrangeas have both pale and pastel components. The color differences are more apparent as you look closely at the details.

PALE COLORS

Pale colors have high value and low saturation, so they will be light but not very bright. It is relatively easy to distinguish between pale and pastel colors with a color chart, but when you are in the garden, the difference is subtle and sometimes more difficult to see. Some flowers may have pale petals and brighter centers or accent or secondary colors, so that they appear to be pastel at certain distances. In fact, as the distance increases, pastel colors will appear to fade to paler hues.

Pale colors may be most appropriately used as background and connecting colors. For this reason, you are likely to find pale colors, such as grayed greens, blues, and reds, in light-valued garden furnishings (trellises, chairs, and pots) and hardscape (pale

stone and wood). Even if such colors start out with more saturation, they often weather to a paler version of the original.

When you think of pale flower and foliage colors, you think of the foliage grays, the pale and grayed blues and greens that can be such a perfect background color for many other flower and foliage colors. You also think of flowers as they begin to bloom; the pale blues of hydrangeas and the pale reds, oranges, and yellows of tulips. Pale also describes flowers past their prime, as their color fades. Roses often fade into pale versions of their original color. Some people insist on removing faded flowers, but these can add interesting variations to the garden's color;

faded petals or leaves on the ground will reflect more light than grass or soil. Even though these colors have little brightness, their lightness is as important as the pastels in creating light and dark compositions, and they won't compete for attention as the higher-saturated colors will.

Like pastels, and perhaps even more so, pale colors are difficult to use in bright sun, in gardens where there are high levels of reflected light because of lighter-colored surroundings, and in large area plantings. They may, however, work well as a background for a more brilliant focal point (an unusual plant or piece of garden furniture or sculpture). In bedding schemes with tall flowers, such as tulips, using shorter pale flowering or foliage plants as underplanting will reflect more light and make the planting scheme noticeable from a greater distance.

Vivid Colors

Vivid colors have high saturation at their natural value level. The basic hues are vivid colors, and if you look at color charts, you will find that in many cases, colors can reach the highest level of saturation at several value levels, so that some hues that are lighter in value may seem more vivid than their basic hue. Many vivid colors in nature are so saturated that they cannot be accurately duplicated in print. If the vivid colors were arranged in a Munsell wheel they would look quite similar to a basic hue circle (see p. 13).

Because vivid colors have high saturation, they are most often noticed first. They are chosen for bedding schemes and gardens that are designed to attract attention. Vivid colors may be used in large expanses that are designed to be seen at a distance, such as some formal parterre designs or highway plantings. They may also be used as small accents in pots or planters to mark entrances.

Light and location play a large part in how vivid a color will look. You can probably remember being in a garden when the light fell on a flower in a way that made the color seem extraordinarily vivid. Often you must stand at just one place to witness such an effect. Even though you may not be aware of it, it is the surrounding colors and the light that contribute to the vividness.

An artist knows how to select background colors that will make a color or colors seem more vivid. This approach can be used by garden designers, too. A color will appear more vivid if it is against less saturated colors, if the lightness and darkness levels of the background are changed, and if complementary or contrasting hues are used. Like all colors, even vivid colors appear grayer in the distance; their visibility depends on the viewing distance and angle, as well as the position and source of light.

The native beautyberry has a beautiful vivid purple berry, which appears in the fall.

Rich red roses merge with their dark foliage yet stand separate from the light-colored garden house. You can see the subtle difference in saturation between the color of the flowers and the more grayed color of the foliage.

RICH COLORS

Rich colors have low value and high saturation; that is, they are dark yet with full color. Generally, rich colors in garden flowers are associated with the red-purples, the blues, and the greens. When yellow and yellow-red become dark, they can appear to be a brown that is called rich, such as certain soil and wood colors.

The hues in rich colors show best close up. If grayed by distance, they lose their impact and tend to become part of the background. In fact, many of the greens found in yews and other green hedge material are often part of the garden structure; they are more saturated than some of the other greens found in the garden, but less saturated than the flower and foliage colors that are intended to be the focus of the garden. In cases where the background is light-colored stone or concrete, the dark rich colors will be either a striking accent or an impressive massed planting.

Because rich colors are so dark, you can include a number of hues and not have the feeling that a garden scene is too busy or has too high a level of contrast. Because the values are all held to the darker levels, there will be a strong sense of unity.

MUTED COLORS

Muted colors have low saturation and medium value;
that is, they are more gray than other colors, and they
are darker than pale colors but lighter than dark
grays. Muted colors are useful in the garden
as a contrast to brightly hued flowers or
foliage, and they can also be used on
their own. Gardens that are
transitional between more striking
gardens, or gardens that have
strongly colored accent or
building features, can use muted
colors as a bridge.

Low saturation means that these
colors will not attract much
attention, particularly if they are
surrounded by colors of higher
saturation, such as pastel, vivid, or rich
colors. If massed, they make an interesting
background, either repeating or contrasting
with a more saturated hue. Muted colors appear
farther away than they really are because grayed colors
tend to appear more distant. Medium value means that
they will appear somewhat more distant than lighter
colors, but closer and larger than darker colors.

Lighting plays a part in muting colors; even the orange
trumpet of a daffodil may appear muted if the light
catches it in a certain way. Overcast skies may gray or
mute many colors. Sunlight falling directly on or
behind certain colors and not on others will make
certain colors look vivid and others more muted.

The muted colors of salvia are low in saturation and medium in value,
making them useful for weaving other colors into a pleasing composition.

BACKGROUND COLORS

The colors of foliage, stone, brick, and mulch form the background colors of the eastern United States landscape and set the scene for garden composition. Learn your local colors; they are the basis for good color composition.

THE ROLE OF
BACKGROUND COLORS

Perhaps the most important colors in the garden are the ones that are rarely discussed in garden color books, the colors that surround the flowers and foliage. These background, or surround, colors are important because they determine how other colors appear. Background colors are the colors of masses of trees and their woody structure, the colors of the sky, the colors of grass, mulch, gravel, and various ground surfaces. These are also the colors of stone, brick, wood, and any manmade background that is seen in or from the garden.

The surrounding colors may vary within a locale, or between locales. Each habitat area has a distinctive color sequence: Pine forests have different colors than hardwood forests, and East Coast forests have different colors than West Coast forests. Dry areas differ from wetlands; uplands from lowlands, and all the grasslands differ. From a designer's viewpoint, a garden that is out of its local color area is often one of the most difficult to design successfully.

Background materials come in a wide range of related colors—mulch, brick, and wood all come in lower-saturated colors that may vary from the warmer hues to the cooler hues. At one time, these materials were restricted primarily to areas in which they occurred naturally or were produced, but now most of these materials are available across the country, and in some cases, internationally. Because these materials surround many of the garden plants, they have a strong influence on the garden's sensed and seen color relationships.

When you begin looking at background colors, you realize that there are color variations in these materials. These variations are small, so you can choose an average color to represent them. Some common background colors are: stone, a medium or dark gray with warm or cool undertones; foliage, a medium green-yellow, low in saturation; brick, a medium yellow-red or red, low in saturation; concrete and aggregate stone, light to medium yellows, low in saturation; terra-cotta, a yellow-red of medium value and saturation; and sky, which varies in color depending on the weather but is often a medium-value blue with some purple in it, often lighter toward the horizon.

These yellow and orange rudbeckias, their green-yellow foliage, and the reddish-purple ornamental grass represent a range of warm colors. The pure hues of the warm colors seen in the circles at right are more easily recognized than their grayed and darkened variations seen in the garden.

COLORS TOGETHER

*T*hrough the years, artists and designers have tried to find regular or mathematical spacing in color systems that would lead them to beautiful color harmonies. Some of these relationships evolved during times when artistic goals were different from modern sensibilities and were based on theories of color vision that have been proven false. Nevertheless, these relationships are still being used as a starting point for developing color combinations.

WARM COLORS

Warm and cool are terms that describe relative sensations for two groups of colors. The warm hues are red, yellow, and magenta or red-purple, with the warmest generally in the red area. Colors that have red in them are generally recognized as being warm in character. Warmth describes a non-visual sensation, but most people have no difficulty understanding the concept and relating it to the color of things they are familiar with, such as fire and the sun. Descriptive terms—hot pinks, fiery reds, sunny yellows—often reflect this apparent relationship.

When gardeners discuss warm and cool colors, such as bright orange flowers against a deep-green hedge background, the comment is made that warm colors advance (appear closer) and cool colors recede (appear farther away). One reason may be that the eye focuses differently when it looks at red than when it looks at green or blue. This refocusing is similar to what happens when the eye looks at objects that are near and far. The eye may focus on red and nearby objects in a similar fashion and on blue and green and far-away objects in a similar fashion. So your eyes feel at rest when you view objects in the distance, as they do when you focus on blue and green. This may account for the idea that green and blue are restful colors.

The apparent ability of warm and cool colors to create different dimensions of distance and depth (sometimes referred to as a color's kinetic ability) is complex, particularly when you start to combine hues of differing values and saturations. Each color has a cool and warm range; that is, for the warm colors, yellow has a warm range moving toward orange and a cool range moving toward green; orange has a warm range moving toward yellow and a cool range moving toward red; and purple has a warm range moving toward red and a cool range moving toward blue. So an orange can appear cooler than a purple, depending on the specific hues involved.

For each of these hue ranges, there is also a range of values (light and dark variations) and a range of saturations (grayed colors). Colors of high value, no matter what the hue, may appear to be closer than medium and low values of the warmest colors. A purple flower, catching the light, may appear lighter and therefore closer than its green foliage. Colors of high saturation, no matter what the hue, may appear to be closer than grayed warm colors. A clear green may appear closer than a medium brown.

Because of the way the eye sees color, people can recognize red, orange, and yellow as warm colors, but may have difficulty deciding whether green-yellow and purple are warm or cool colors. The visual signals for the last two colors may vary, depending upon whether there is more yellow or green, or more red or blue, apparent in the hue. Green-yellow foliage with a purple-pink flower may send mixed visual messages; so it may not always be possible to predict whether a warm color will advance, even if it is next to a cool color.

Warm colors are used for reasons other than their ability to stretch or contract distance. Many people do think they feel warmer in the presence of yellow, red, or magenta, and so in a cooler climate or during cooler times of the year, these colors may be used to heat up a garden. Think of gardens outside living-area windows during early spring and late fall and winter, and imagine the impact of the warmer colors, whether they are yellows and oranges in spring bulbs or yellows and reds in autumn leaves.

Pink impatiens and green coleus leaves—the words lead you to expect to see warm-colored flowers against cool-colored foliage, as in the first set of color samples. But because the pink is a cool pink (it has purple or blue in it) and the green is a warm green (it has yellow in it), what you see is closer to the second set of samples. The combination strikes an unexpected balance.

COOL COLORS

Cool colors have blue in them. The cool colors are green, blue, and violet, with the coolest in the blue-green area. Like warmth, coolness is a nonvisual attribute, but the association with water and ice seems to reinforce the connection between sight and sensation.

Like the warm colors, the cool colors have a range of warmth and coolness. Green appears warmer toward its yellow range and cooler toward its blue range; blue appears warmer toward its green range and cooler toward its purple range; purple appears warmer toward its red range and cooler toward its blue range. This range of coolness and warmth is particularly interesting for the greens, because of the abundance of green foliage in gardening. Since most foliage is green-yellow, even small shifts toward the green and blue sides of the hue circle make a plant look bluish, particularly when the colors are less saturated. Instead of thinking of greens as being yellow-green and blue-green, think of them as being warm and cool greens, and you will realize some new design possibilities for foliage as well as flower gardens.

The attribute of value is also important in the considerations of the cool colors, again because of the abundance of green in the garden. Remember that a light color may be more eye-catching or

The cool colors usually associated with foliage in the garden can range from the green-yellows of hosta leaves to the greens that appear to have some blue or purple in them, as in the ajuga.

appear nearer than even a warm color, if the warm color is darker or grayed. Because the pure hues of green, blue, and purple are lower on the relative value scale, they can be lightened even more than the warm colors without losing their identity. Cool colors make a number of very good tints. There are light cool flowers and light cool foliage; they are usually complex combinations of colors, including variegation, that create the effect best at a distance.

Cool colors are considered easier to live with than warm colors, so most gardens and landscapes have the advantage of being considered restful whether they are designed or not. However, the unrelieved repetition of greens and blues can be monotonous; even restfulness needs some variation to keep its effect. This means including other colors in your garden, whether from flower, foliage, or hardscape.

Cool colors are popular in hot climates. The apparent coolness of a predominantly green and blue landscape can be appreciated from within buildings as well as by people in the garden.

ANALOGOUS COLORS

Analogous colors are colors that are closely related on the color wheel. Analogous colors are next to or near each other on the circle; if you think of the color solid, they are the colors next to each other on the outside, their grayed hues moving inward like a wedge. The colors may share a common hue, such as yellow, yellow-red, and red, or green-yellow, green, and green-blue. Analogous color schemes, other than the greens, rarely exist in the garden. When you read about analogous combinations in garden writing, the designers are focusing on flower colors, not the overall color composition that you see.

The concept of analogous colors is still a useful one, since many gardeners find the combination of closely related flower colors pleasing. To define the colors that you plan to use in your design, start at one point on the color wheel and choose one or two colors to the left or right. Then add the light and dark and gray variations of those hues. You will see that tremendous variations can be achieved.

An interesting aspect of such color schemes is that from a distance, colors that are related can look very similar; you get the visual impact of a mass planting of a single color. When you move closer, the plantings will look more varied, and the individual colors will become visible. As people move through the garden, they see the plants and flowers in different ways.

Colors that are related to each other on the hue circle, such as the yellows and yellow-reds of the marigold flowers, are considered to be analogous colors.

COMPLEMENTARY COLORS

Complementary colors are colors that have the greatest amount of hue contrast. On a color wheel, they are the colors opposite each other. In the color solid, they are the colors arrayed in a straight line through its center (and therefore including the grayed hues). When you mix complements additively (light), the result is white or neutral gray; when you mix two complements subtractively (pigment), the result is black or neutral gray. At one time it was thought that if you took a painting and spun it as an optical-mixing disk spins (see p. 25), if the apparent color was gray, you had achieved a balanced composition.

Due to some confusion in naming and using different materials, you will sometimes read that orange is the complement of blue and yellow is the complement of purple, but color systems that have a scientific basis place yellow opposite blue. To make this issue still more confusing, the color opposite yellow on the Munsell wheel is called purple-blue, but if you look at it, it is the color recognized by most people as blue.

As a practical consideration, it is rare in garden design to find a simple complementary color scheme; more colors are usually involved. Because garden writing almost always refers to color as flower color, schemes that are called complementary usually focus on flower color and ignore foliage and other background colors.

Some other combinations related to complementary colors are split complements, analogous complements, and double complements. Split complements combine one color with the two colors next to (surrounding) the complementary color. The split complements of green are purple and red; the split complements of green-yellow are purple-blue and red-purple. Analogous complements combine two related colors with the complement of one of the colors, such as green and green-yellow with purple. Double complements combine related colors with both of their complements, such as green and blue-green with red and red-purple.

Complementary color schemes are often suggested because they are considered more visually exciting than other schemes, since they contain extremes of hue contrast. This is true at high levels of saturation, but if value and saturation are held constant (all light or dark colors or all grayed colors), the appearance changes dramatically. Background or surrounding colors play an important part in determining how the complements are seen.

This color scheme relates the near-complementary colors of the purplish-blue and orangish-yellow flowers. Seen up close, this design portrays the dramatic appeal of such colors used together.

Triads are groups of three colors that are equally spaced around the hue circle. Such a triad forms the basis for this combination of reddish-yellow rudbeckia with the bluish-green of the foliage and the reddish-purple of the coleus. Although you are probably more familiar with the term as used with pure hues (sample at top), such combinations are not common in the garden. The triad relationship holds even when saturation and value are altered, as in the samples below.

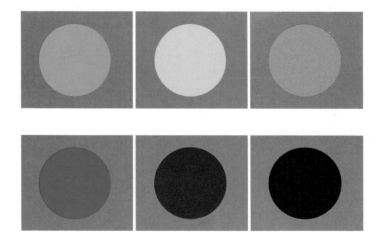

Triads and Tetrads

Triads are combinations of three colors that are equidistant from each other on the color wheel. Triads (and tetrads) were developed with the artist's color wheel, which has six or twelve basic colors. When using the Munsell wheel, which has ten basic colors, triadic (and tetradic) colors still exist, as do the relationships, but are not named as basic hues. One triad that uses bluish-green (a common foliage color) as a starting point is shown at the top of the facing page. The colors at full saturation appear quite contrasting; when the sequences are changed in value and saturation, as shown at the bottom of the facing page (a lighter, grayer group of the same hues and a darker, grayer group of the same hues), the relationships seem to be more interesting to gardeners.

Tetrads are combinations of four colors that are equidistant from each other on the color wheel. If you use green as a starting point, the other colors in the combination become a yellow-red, a red-purple, and a blue. At their full saturation, they don't seem to have much attraction for garden designers, but the grayed high-value combination and the grayed low-value combination looks very like some garden schemes.

In addition to these schemes, which are based on paint mixing, there are combinations or sequences of colors based on the colors' position in the color solid. It is possible to draw imaginary lines through the color solid that are diagonal, spiral, or discrete (broken at regular intervals) to form the basis of different and interesting color relationships.

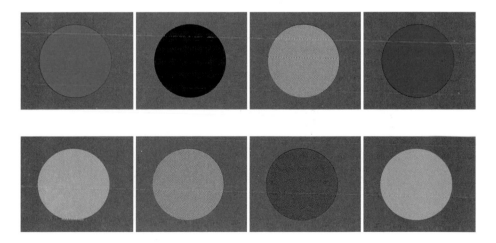

Tetrads are groups of four colors that are equally spaced around the hue circle, here seen in various saturations and values.

AMOUNT AND PLACEMENT OF COLOR

The amount and placement of color are quite important in how that color is perceived. In a garden, where people can move through and around plantings and can view plants from higher and lower vantage points, the color composition they see is constantly changing. Some classic gardens were meant to be seen from one particular place. Often garden designers will consider one view of the garden to be the most important for setting the garden structure—a view from a main living area inside the house or a view from a porch or deck to a back garden or a view when approaching a house. In most cases, these views are primary views, but they are not the only view, so the garden designer needs to consider all vantage points before making design decisions.

Equal amounts of colors, particularly if they share equal value and saturation, can be exciting, disturbing, or tiring. The easiest visual analogy is to think of a checkerboard effect, where the eye moves from color to color without settling or focusing in any particular place on the composition. This rarely occurs in a real garden because of the complexity of the visual field, but when equal amounts of two or more flower colors are used, as in some classic bedding schemes, a distinctly checkerboard or polka-dot effect is the result.

Varying the amount and proportion of color seems to offer more interest and scope for design manipulation. Think about the different impacts of a color scheme that is mostly yellow with a little red as opposed to one that is mostly red with a little yellow. Varying the value and saturation can make the differences become even more dramatic or less noticeable. Manipulating the viewing conditions, light, and distance will offer even more variety.

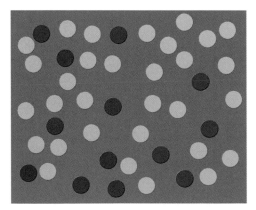 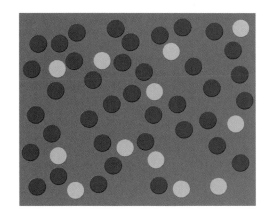

Imagine these circles as red and yellow tulips on a green background and you begin to see how thinking conceptually about color can helps you plan your design. For example, you can see immediately if you prefer regular spacing, more red, or more yellow.

Most gardens are inviting displays that offer the opportunity to see colors from different vantage points. As you move through the garden, pay attention to changes in the amount and placement of the colors you see, and note your reaction to those changes.

HOW COLOR IS SEEN

*H*ow we see and then interpret colors is
a fascinating study of physical and emotional
reactions. Scientists have devoted much attention
to the mystery of color perception. Artists
and designers need to understand these perceptual
effects, at least in a general way, in order to
manipulate them to create beautiful gardens.

PERCEPTION

*E*veryone sees color differently. You are probably most aware of the differences in people's emotional reactions to color. In extreme cases, people may restrict themselves to using only certain colors; painting only in blues, dressing only in black, or gardening only with flowers in pale drifts of color. Most people are not so rigid in their color preferences, but emotional ties can be confusing as reasons to justify the use of color. For example, purple is often called a regal color because long ago it was worn by royalty or wealthy persons, but it is also the color of spiked hairdos and small children's toys and clothes. Red is a color that is supposed to be avoided completely on hospital walls because of its emotional and physical reactions, and yet you see masses of red flowers blooming outside hospitals, and patients and doctors apparently enjoy the effect. Yellow is thought of as cheerful and bright, yet many of the colors on the yellow hue page in the Munsell book seem drab and dull. It was thought for many years that only natural colors were suitable for foodstuffs; pure blues or violets were considered

unappetizing. Now you see "blue" potatoes and corn chips (although it's about as accurate a description as most blue flowers) and gelatin desserts in the most amazing range of blues and purples.

What all this suggests is that the emotional content of color can be manipulated in many ways, and if you base your designs only on emotional content, the success or failure of your work may be a matter of someone else's personal preference. While this is not a problem in home landscape design, and in fact, many very good home gardens are built around very personal color combinations, as a generalization, such choices will limit the appeal of your design.

Relatively little study has been devoted to finding out if some of the color preferences and guidelines for color use in other artistic and design fields, such as interior design, architectural design, food, textile design, or furniture design, have any relation to preferences and emotional reactions to the colors used in the outdoor landscape. People have a universal awareness of colors, but not a universal response to color meaning. In all languages there are color words, indicating that all people are aware of color in some fashion. Studies have shown that after black and white, red is the color word that is used most often, followed by green and yellow, blue, brown, and finally purple, pink, orange, and gray. There is no proof that color preferences transcend cultural, social, and physical boundaries. Diversity of opinion is a fact.

There are physical limitations in the way people see color. Complete color blindness, or the ability to see only differences in light and dark, is rare. Partial color blindness usually takes the form of an inability to see the colors of red and green, or more rarely, blue and yellow. Finally, people may be said to have abnormal color vision when colors are seen, but the individuals have difficulty mixing or matching colors as others do.

People also differ in their ability to perceive subtle color differences. Less then half of the population can discriminate between colors at a fine enough level to be employed in jobs where tasks are color-determined. Although this limitation may be more critical in industrial applications than in design, it is interesting to note that few, if any, art and design schools test for either color blindness or fine color discrimination.

Other physical limitations result from age, health, and fatigue. As people age, their vision slightly yellows (people who have had cataract surgery can often see a noticeable change in the repaired eye) and certain diseases reduce color discrimination temporarily or permanently. Prolonged exposure to strong sunlight can temporarily reduce color discrimination as well; this is important information for gardeners, who spend a lot of time outdoors. Finally, it is always worth remembering that even if they have normal color vision, no two people can be said to see color in the same way. When you know this, do not be discouraged that the study of color will be a study in frustration, but adopt a more understanding outlook about color composition. When people disagree with you about color, it is wise to listen to what they say; they may see something that you do not.

Even though we see colors differently, every person's visual system has the same purpose: to provide information by identifying the surroundings. To identify an object, your eyes separate it from the background by enhancing the color differences in the scene. This process is selective; people unconsciously notice what they want to see and ignore what seems unimportant. Perhaps you have been on garden tours where people right next to you ignored a plant that you thought was very beautiful; they were not attuned to your interests and knowledge, and so missed seeing the plant until it was pointed out to them. In fact, one of the aims of garden design is to focus attention on certain aspects of the garden, acting as a kind of spotlight. Focus is critical to perception.

It is generally accepted that reds advance and blues recede. Without the depth cues from the lower picture, you might not believe that the blue color card is so far in front of the red.

Because the critical task of vision is identifying objects, most people ignore or play down the effects of lighting changes. This unconscious correction is called color constancy, and it's one way your visual system takes an environment that is constantly changing and makes it appear stable. Color constancy makes everyday life easier; you don't have to wonder if the plant that looks dark in the shade is the same plant that you saw in the sun; you know that it is, and rarely even pause to think about these differences.

What you see in art and optical-illusion books are the extreme cases of these perceptual adjustments that your eye makes to help you identify your surroundings—they are startling and fun, and often you can't believe your own eyes. The reason that these studies are presented as squares or circles is to remove as many other influences as is practical, so that you can focus your attention on color. These two-dimensional squares and circles are useful, but they have their limitations. Since gardening is a three-dimensional art form, three-dimensional models to study color can be even more intriguing tools. As you play with various combination of colors, you can see how colors look next to and surrounding each other. You can manipulate your models in other ways as well. For example, you could change the lighting, having some objects in sun and some in shade; you could alter the saturation and value of the colors to be more garden-like; or you could change the background colors. Any such alterations will help increase your visual understanding of how colors behave in the garden.

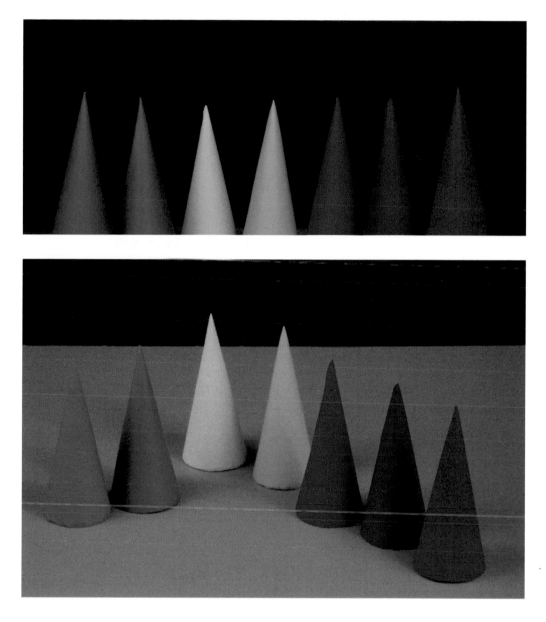

Models are useful for studying the effects of distance and color. You probably would not guess from the top photo alone that the yellow cone is so far behind the other cones.

For the garden designer, it is more practical to think of these effects as influences than tricks. Being able to predict the direction of the changes and to understand why they may change the garden's appearance is a useful design skill.

There are four adjustments that you routinely encounter when learning about color. The first is simultaneous contrast, where colors are influenced by other colors directly surrounding them and the color differences are emphasized. The next is successive contrast, where colors are influenced by colors seen immediately beforehand and produce the effect known as afterimages. The third is color assimilation, sometimes known as the spreading effect or the Von Bezold effect, where very small areas of color that are touching appear more alike (the opposite effect of simultaneous contrast). The last is color separation, when colors that are separated by some distance but are within the visual field appear to be more alike.

These four adjustments rarely occur singly. One purpose of discussing them separately is to help you learn to focus on one color problem at a time. Then you can see how the adjustments interact. If you practice observing these effects in different situations, you will learn to predict how colors will react together in your garden design.

SIMULTANEOUS CONTRAST

When a color is surrounded by a different color, both colors change in appearance. These changes cannot be measured by instruments, but are very powerful visual effects nonetheless. Colors can shift in hue, value, and saturation, though the value shift is, as always, most noticed.

You can predict which colors will be affected and how: Smaller areas of color change more than larger areas of color, and intermediate or complex colors change in appearance more than basic hues. The hue will shift away from the background color (as you imagine the hues spaced around the color wheel), except when the background is a complementary color; then there will be little shift in hue, but the color will increase in saturation. The value of a color will seem higher (lighter) if the background is dark and lower (darker) if the background is light. The saturation of a color will seem greater (a brighter color) if the background is grayed and less (a grayed color) if the background is saturated.

Colors shift because your eyes try to emphasize the difference between colors, so if you remember how colors are arranged around the color wheel and in the color solid, you can predict the direction of the color shift. For example, you'll know how to make a red-purple appear more red or more blue, darker or lighter, or more gray or more pure in hue.

Underplanting is one way to alter the background color of a flowering display. Here, yellow tulips are seen against the blue and green background of forget-me-nots instead of brown mulch.

Garden designers will often take a plant in a pot and move it around the garden, leaving it there to see how the plant looks in various settings and lighting conditions. This is an easy and accurate way to study the effects of combining colors. If you want the color of a plant to change appearance in hue, value, or saturation, you can do this by altering the background or moving the plant so it has a different background. One way this is done is by placing groundcovers or low plants below a taller bulb, perennial, or shrub. This underplanting can alter the background from the usual mulch or green groundcover to any of a number of colors. It is particularly effective in flowering displays. Some examples are blue lobelia or white alyssum under flowering tulips and white mazus under roses.

If you are exhibiting flowers or considering plants as color accents, it is very important to know how they will be displayed—upon what background and under what light source. A plant placed against the wrong background may look dull and insignificant. When you are interested in fine color differences, such as in flower judging or comparing two cultivars that are very close in color, a similar color background will make small color differences more noticeable. When the background for both plants is a very different color, other characteristics, such as form and texture, become more noticeable.

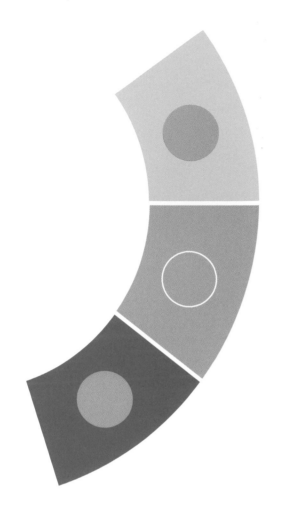

SIMULTANEOUS CONTRAST—HUE

Hue shift is easiest to see when the hues are at a relatively high level of saturation; once you have seen the effect and identified it, it will be easier to recognize in the garden, where the hues will not be as saturated. If you use the color wheel as reference and can accurately identify both the object color and its background, you can predict how the hues will shift. The shift will be to the right or to the left around the color wheel, as the color moves away from the background color. The exception is when the complementary color is the background; then the color will appear at a relatively high level of saturation. That is, green-yellow can look either more yellow or more green depending upon its background. As the background colors change around the hue circle, you can see the green-yellow appearing more yellow when it has a green or blue-green background and more green when it has a yellow or yellow-red background. When green-yellow is placed on purple (its complement), it does not shift in hue, but appears at its most saturated.

Hue shifts in appearance as the background color changes. Green-yellow may appear more yellow on a green background and more green on a yellow background. Red-purple may appear to be more red or more purple.

Similarly, red-purple can look either more red or more purple, depending on its background. When it is on red or yellow-red, it looks more purple, and when it is on blue or blue-green, it looks more red. When it is on green (its complement), it is at its highest apparent saturation.

Green-yellow is a typical color of foliage in the garden. When you put green-yellow on the colors that represent those found as backgrounds in the garden (terra-cotta, foliage, concrete, sky, and brick), the hue shift is difficult to discern. It is a much more subtle effect, and until your eye is attuned to it, you may not even be aware of any hue shift. Nevertheless, you should be able to see that when next to the sky color, the green-yellow looks more yellow; on the brick, the green-yellow appears very little affected in hue.

TERRA-COTTA

FOLIAGE

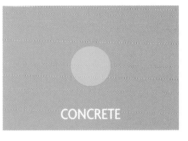

CONCRETE

SKY

BRICK

The green-yellow circle, representing the color of foliage, shifts relatively little in hue when seen against garden background colors.

SIMULTANEOUS CONTRAST-VALUE

The only way to show the effect of a change in value without involving hue or saturation is to use the achromatic colors: black, white, and gray. When the background color is black, all hues will appear lighter; if the background color is white, all hues will appear darker. When the background color is a medium gray, the hues that are higher in value (yellow, yellow-red, green-yellow) appear lighter; the hues that are lower in value (purple and blue) appear darker, and the colors that are in the middle value range appear unaffected.

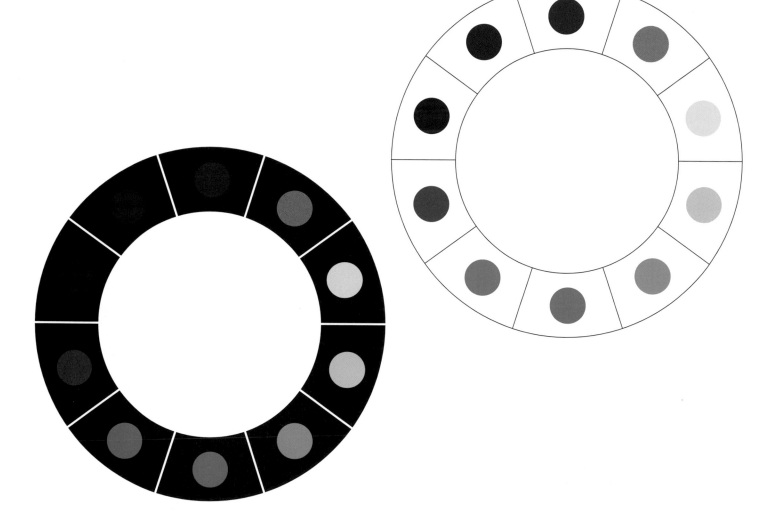

The basic hues, seen on backgrounds of low, high, and middle values (black, white, and middle gray). On the dark background, the colors appear lighter; on the light background, the colors appear darker.

In a garden, however, hues are rarely seen against achromatic black, white, or gray, so you have to consider them against the usual garden background colors. Colors seen against dark green, dark brick, or stone will appear lighter; colors seen against concrete or lighter-colored brick and stone will appear darker. Remember, however, that in the garden value shift cannot be analyzed by itself, in isolation. There will also be a hue shift because a hedge is not only dark but also dark and green.

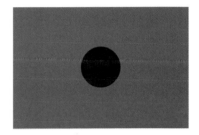

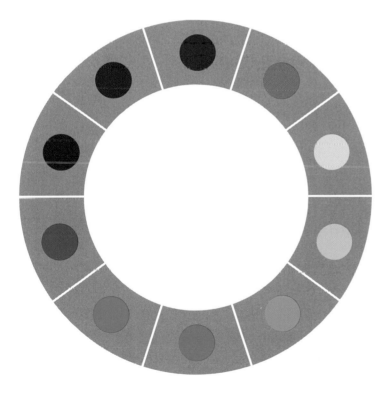

Purple, the darkest hue, almost disappears when seen against the dark background colors of the garden.

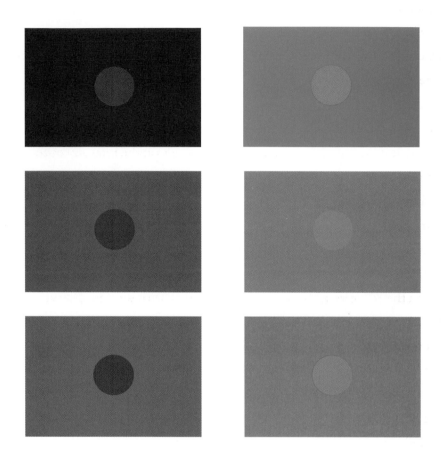

A color of mid-level saturation can change appearance if the
backgrounds are a pure color or very grayed. The red and green circles
look very gray in the top squares, where they are seen against their pure
hues. In the bottom squares, where they are seen against near grays,
the circles look quite saturated.

SIMULTANEOUS CONTRAST—SATURATION

If the background color is grayer, or of lower saturation, colors will appear more saturated or pure in hue; if the background is highly saturated, colors will appear grayer, or less saturated. Many of the traditional background colors in the garden are of low saturation, so flower colors, which are nearly always more saturated, appear brighter and receive more attention. Backgrounds are not always less saturated, however, particularly in urban and suburban gardens. Surfaces such as painted trim on houses and garden ornaments, commercial buildings, art, and signs with bright colors are some examples of high-saturation backgrounds. In such situations, you might look for plantings in colors that are less saturated than the background. Rather than competing, the planting will enhance the saturated colors and allow the building, sign, or art to be the focus of attention.

SUCCESSIVE CONTRAST

When you stare at a colored object for a period of time and then shift your eyes away, you see the complementary color of the object. This is called an afterimage, and most people are not aware of this adjustment that your visual system makes because it is a fleeting effect that can be seen most clearly against a blank sheet of white paper. (You may have seen the illusion in which you stare at a green, black, and orange version of the American flag and then shift your gaze to a blank page, where you glimpse a red, white, and blue afterimage of the flag.) If, however, you look at a certain color and then immediately move to a different-colored background, the next color you see is a mixture of the complement of the first color and the background color. The duration of the afterimage depends on the intensity of the initial color and the length of viewing time, as well as on the eye's ability to adapt. The brighter the colors and the larger the area of color, the stronger this effect will be.

If you are in a green garden and move to a garden where the flowers are a complementary purple-red, the red flowers may look brighter and the green foliage grayer because of the effect of the afterimage. If you are inside a dark house and move outside to the garden, the garden may look lighter because of the effect of the afterimage. So successive contrast may be useful in helping you design transitional areas, where people move from one garden to another. The word "successive" reminds you that the colors you have just seen influence the colors you see next.

COLOR ASSIMILATION

Now instead of looking at large areas of color, such as the circles in the last section, consider smaller areas of color. In the garden, think of smaller flowers or leaves or flowers seen at a distance. When colors occupy a relatively small area of the retina, the effect of simultaneous contrast reverses itself. Colors that appeared to be most different now seem to look more alike. This effect is called color assimilation.

The effect is best known from its application in textiles. Tapestry and rug designers discovered that changing the color of single threads in a repeat design would change the apparent colors of the overall design, sometimes quite

dramatically. Perhaps the effect has been noted by gardeners as well, since certain plants are called "weavers" and are used in joining and mixing colors.

What occurs in color assimilation is that the small areas of color form an average of the original colors, an optical mix in which the hue, value, and saturation of the color seen is an average of the hue, value, and saturation of the component colors. In this instance, colors that are complementary do not make each other appear brighter or more saturated; they combine to make a color that approaches gray. Colors that are analogous will often appear more similar; if they are close in value, they may even appear to shimmer.

When the areas of color are relatively small, complementary colors seen together seem less brilliant. If you place this page at a distance greater than the normal reading distance, such as on the floor, the graying is intensified, as the colors mix optically.

Color assimilation is often seen in a single plant. Veins in leaves and margins in flowers that are different colors affect the color of the plant as a whole when seen from a distance where the details cannot be discerned. If the veins are lighter and yellowish, as in many trees, the leaves will look lighter and more green-yellow. If the veins are darker and reddish, then the leaves will look darker and more gray.

Color assimilation also affects plant groupings, especially if the plants are of fine texture. A plant such as *Verbena bonariensis,* which is a dark purple, can make the whole scene look darker and less saturated when seen from a distance. This is the opposite effect that it has when seen up close, where its purple color may provide contrast that makes the surrounding colors appear lighter and more saturated. Smaller groups of plants may show up when seen from nearby, but when the distance increases, the colors will start to mix, and an unforeseen color may result. That's why you need to know what the viewing distance will be when you mass your plant groupings.

A change in value of a small area can make a startling difference in the overall color. Here, the narrow white lines make the colors of the basic hue circle seem lighter than they are. When the same hues are combined with narrow black lines, the colors seem darker.

The colors of the pink and white cleome are seen here against a varied background. The different pinks look more alike when seen against the green foliage and less similar when seen against the other pink flowers.

SEPARATED COLORS

When colors are not touching each other, they tend to look more alike. This is probably one of the reasons that so called single-color gardens are so successful; if the flower colors were placed directly touching one another, you would realize the great range of individual colors. But because they are more often separated in the visual field by the greens of foliage and the other background colors, the overall impression is of visual unity, where one color group dominates. This perceptual relationship can also help you when you have a particularly difficult color or color group to deal with; an easy solution may be to make sure that the two colors are not visually touching each other.

One of the most common design problems is with house and trim colors. If these are difficult as direct background, plant hedges or other colors that vary in hue, value, or saturation next to the house, and then proceed with your plantings, using the green of the hedges as a background. Imagine the situation in which you want to plant red in front of a brick house. When you see the red flower against the red brick, the differences in the reds will be accentuated. But if you plant a green hedge between the house and the flowers, the red of the flowers will be seen against the green of the hedge, instead of clashing with the brick.

Most gardeners, focusing on the flowers, would call this an orange or red garden. On closer examination, the complex blending and separating of the flower and foliage colors become apparent.

FASHION AND MARKETING

In the world of fashion and architecture, colors fade in and out of popularity. That's true of plant and flower colors as well, although introductions of new flowering or display plants are not usually based on any relation of their color to current popular colors. This can cause design problems, since to display a new plant introduction successfully, you may have to harmonize its color with not only the local color (that is, the colors of the trees, shrubs, and herbaceous plants that are generally found in the local landscape), but with current and emerging colors that are fashionable in the exterior or interior architectural fields.

Color marketing in the plant business seems to take place primarily at the grower level; the plants that you see in wholesale catalogs are the ones that get to the mass market via the growers at all levels. Often the primary reason for a new introduction's success is more its qualities of cultivation than its ability to be part of a color design. Nevertheless, there are many new colors that are available each season. As with all color marketing, the naming of the colors of new plants is important to their image, even though it may not relate closely to the actual color of the flower or foliage.

Color marketing groups, whose members are trained in color arts and sciences, set color trends and forecast color trends for industry, manufactured products, and services. One such association is the Color Marketing Group, an international association of color designers who forecast color directions one to three years in advance for products in the following areas: residential, transportation, architectural/building, fashion, communications/graphics, recreational, and environments for retail, hospitality, office, and health care. Colors for the general consumer or residential marketplace are forecast in the spring, and colors for contract or commercial markets are forecast each fall.

New plant introductions are constantly changing the color landscape. Recent All-American selections include (clockwise from top) Petunia F1 *'Fantasy Pink Morn' (1996),* Zinnia angustifolia *'Crystal White' (1997),* Rudbeckia hirta *'Indian Summer' (1995), and* Celosia cristata *'Prestige Scarlet' (1997).*

COLOR IN CONTEXT

*A*fter learning the basic color vocabulary and its relation to how people perceive colors, the practical designer will be eager to move out into the garden and put this new knowledge to work. Once in the garden, however, the designer realizes quickly that color can not be evaluated in isolation; the context in which it is seen must also be considered. Additional information about light and texture is needed. Comparing color mixtures, the garden designer further understands that color is not static; plants and landscapes age and alter their appearance in a continuing kaleidoscope of hue, value, and saturation.

*Cherry blossoms around the Tidal Basin in Washington, D.C.,
in the delicate light of dawn.*

LIGHT

Most gardeners focus their attention on the color of their plants and see but don't notice the colors of light in their garden and larger landscape. However, once you begin to see how light changes in color and intensity and can predict how it will change the way your garden looks, it will be a constant part of your color awareness.

When you're out in the garden during the day, you may think of light as coming from two sources, the sun and the sky. Sunlight is more direct yellow light; skylight is more diffused blue light. As light enters the atmosphere, the blue wavelengths are scattered out and seen as the blue skylight. The sunlight is the sum of the remaining wavelengths, which equal yellow light. If you recall the discussion of additive color mixing (see p. 23), you know that yellow light and blue light are complements. When added together, they form white light, which is the color of light before it enters the atmosphere. If you look carefully, you can see the effects of these light sources in your surroundings. Look at a tree, such as an oak or maple, whose leaves are green-yellow (although we call the color "green"). The leaves that face the sun are yellow—this is the color of the light from the sun. The leaves that face away from the sun are more bluish—this is the color of the light from the sky.

Other light that you see all around you is light that is modified as it either passes through an object or is reflected back from an object. The colors that we see are a result of the sunlight, the skylight, the light that is reflected back from specific objects, and the color of the object. Such examples are all around us. When you stand under a tree in early spring, the light is bright green-yellow from the yellow sunlight traveling through and reflecting from the new leaves. Light is reflected more than once. When you see a complex object such as a tree with leaves and branches, the light is reflected back and forth from one surface to another, creating a wonderful depth of color detail that cannot be duplicated in any other medium. Looking anywhere in your garden, you can see these naturally occurring progressions of color, called "color sequences," if you are aware of the color of the light, as well as the color of the objects.

Without light, there is no color. Imagine yourself out in the garden before the sun rises. At first, you can see nothing. As light appears, you can discern light and dark, then recognize shapes, and as more light appears, you begin to recognize colors around you. As the light increases, you can distinguish more and more colors, and those colors change as the light from the sun and the sky changes. You remain in the garden, and if the light becomes too bright, again you cannot discern colors clearly; everything is white or white-yellow. The sun moves in the sky, and again you can see a full range of color. As the sun sinks lower in the sky, the sequence is reversed; colors slowly disappear, then you can see only light and dark, and finally, nothing.

Every day, light from the sun and the sky changes how your garden looks. If you can think about the intensity and the color of the light in your garden in terms of additive color mixing, you will be able to predict how the colors in the garden will look at any time of day. In the early morning, the light is often reddish or pinkish; there is less dust and pollution in the air, and so colors seem clearer and more saturated. At midday, the light may seem yellow, blue, or white, depending upon the cloud cover and dust or pollution. In the evening, the

Sequences of color seen at different times of day. As the color, direction, and angle of the light change, the gradations reveal the complex colors of "pink" cherry blossoms.

Reflected light is a powerful influence on the colors of objects. It is easier to see the changed colors on the light-colored urn and the neutral gray background than on the dark green ivy.

light returns to reddish, with some orange or purple, depending upon the dust, the pollution, and the clouds. The colors of light reveal the size of the particles in the atmosphere that are scattering the light; from the smallest to the largest particles the colors will range from blue to yellow to red to white.

There are devices that can measure both the intensity and color of the light, but your eyes are only aware of relative differences in light, and so it is sufficient for gardeners to talk about relative changes in intensity or color. Because of this variation in the intensity and color of light, different colors are more visible at different times of day. When the light is low, as at the end of the day, greens and blues will appear brighter while the reds become darker as your eyes shift from day to night vision. Our eyes are most sensitive to greenish-yellow. In average daylight, red is the most visible or eye-catching color, along with yellow and yellow-red, followed by green and then blue and purple. Any color that is high in value will be more visible in low light, and colors that are more saturated will be seen more clearly than those that are less saturated.

Daylight

When you're trying to match colors to color swatches, such as trying to match the color of a flower to the Munsell or RHS charts (see pp. 8-10), you are advised to use north light, usually with a high overcast, not direct sunlight or deep shade. This light, called standard daylight, can be mimicked by certain indoor lights and is considered a basic standard viewing condition. This light is also considered ideal for garden photography, particularly when the purpose is to convey the color of a given flower or foliage. However, a plant's color as seen under these conditions is only a very small part of the plant's color as it is seen every day in the landscape.

When the light source is indirect or diffused, it may be easier to see the so-called true color of an object. It is the proper lighting for color matching, but there is less value and saturation contrast. This means that the color scheme is less likely to grab attention, so other measures must be taken to compensate. If the light where you live is not generally strong and direct and you want to direct attention to certain colors, you will want to compensate by massing color to attract attention, by using strong forms and good garden structure, and by using more saturated colors.

Other atmospheric conditions can influence the color and intensity of daylight. In areas with high humidity, the light seems less clear because it scatters every time it touches a drop of moisture. Most people are very aware of the clearness of the light in arid climates, such as the southwestern United States. In hazy light, dark colors tend to be somewhat bluish, and objects seem farther away than they actually are. Lighter objects are not as affected, and objects that are relatively close by do not seem to be affected at all. Light-colored objects in the middle distance appear a little more brown or red. In a mist, colors nearby appear darker or purer; at a distance, they fade into white. Snow acts like mist because white light is added, sometimes in large amounts. Fog is similar to haze, but not ordinarily blue in color. You may not be able to see objects at all, or they may be surrounded by light if the light source is strong enough.

In direct lighting, such as strong sunlight in a very clear atmosphere, the hue shifts toward yellow or blue, and the values and the saturation are increased. This means that value and saturation contrasts can be very great, and your eye can be attracted to many objects. One of the difficulties in designing gardens in such light may be having too much contrast. Value contrast is more noticeable than hue or saturation contrast.

The direction the light comes from is also important. Photographers know this, and refer to backlighting (where the sun is shining through the back of the object), side lighting (where the sun is shining on the side of the object), and front lighting (in which the light is behind the observer, shining directly on the object). The movement of the sun alone changes the lighting on a garden. Choosing your garden orientation with the path of the sun in mind results in wonderful three-dimensional effects. Designing a garden that can be viewed from several vantage points enhances the effect even further. All other art forms try to reproduce this effect or its emotional result. From a color standpoint, taking advantage of such lighting increases the range of color that you see.

Look closely at your garden at different times of day, as the light changes in direction, color, and intensity. As the months pass, you will discover hidden beauty in these subtle shifts.

Lotus flowers lit from various directions. Directional lighting adds drama by increasing the range of colors that you see. Front lighting (top right) produces the least amount of color variation.

In winter, the light of the blue sky is reflected from the snow-covered landscape, lending a bluish cast to this scene.

SEASONAL LIGHT

Everyone is aware that light changes with the seasons. In summer, when most gardens are at their peak, the sun is high in the sky and the light looks white-yellow. In fall and spring, when the sun is lower in the sky, the light must pass through more of the earth's atmosphere and therefore is scattered more, creating more reds, oranges, purples, and blues. In winter, when the sun is at its lowest point, the light is not as intense, so contrasts are not as great as in summer. You are, however, aware of the value contrasts that result from the low level of the sun, which are roughly the equivalent of side lighting.

As the seasons change, there is also a striking change in the reflected light in the landscape. In spring, the new leaves are relatively thin, so a great deal more light can pass through the leaves and be reflected by the leaves; it is nearly the equivalent of having green-yellow lights shine down on you. This powerful effect colors the entire landscape.

In summer, in addition to the reflected green from foliage on trees and shrubs, there is light reflected from flowers. When the foliage colors turn to red, orange, and yellow in the fall, the reflected light is the mixture of these colors. As the leaves fall on the ground, the same colors are also reflected back, intensifying the whole picture. In winter, snow reflects the blue light of the sky. Photographers and printers prefer to color-correct images of snowscapes because people expect to see white snow (because of color constancy), but with some effort, you can see the reflected light in such landscapes.

The green-yellows of spring foliage can be seen reflected in the water
(top). The colors that you see reflected in the water are also reflected in
the landscape. In fall, the reflected light takes on the red, orange, and
yellow cast of the autumn foliage (above).

A sunny spot of color will appear very light when it is framed by deep shade.

SHADE AND SUN

Shade is another type of indirect lighting outside. But instead of light being scattered, as in the overcast blue sky or haze or fog, an object blocks the light of the sun yet allows the blue light of the sky to be seen. This creates shade, and although most people think of shade as black, in fact the light that makes up shade is blue, the light from the sky. Blue may not be the predominant color of shade if other colored objects nearby are highly reflective, such as a brick building or tree leaves, or if the day is not clear. But color is not the most salient feature of shade. Relative lightness and

darkness are more important to most gardeners. So gardeners tend to talk about shade in terms of value differences: high shade, dappled shade, and dark shade.

High shade, so called because it describes the shade under trees that have limbs beginning from relatively high off the ground, has a relatively high level of light intensity. There is the light left over from the sun and the sky (only a portion of the light has been blocked), and the light that is being reflected from objects in the area. It is easier to grow plants in high shade than in dark shade, and because of this relatively large amount of reflected light, it is easier to see colors too.

The color of the mayapple flower in shade is actually darker than the color of its leaf in the sun, but we still think of it as a white flower with dark green foliage.

Dappled shade describes darkness that is intermittent; that is, you see light in some places and dark in some places, usually as a result of light streaming between and among trees. Such light can be quite pleasant, but if the value differences are too great, as on a very sunny day, it can be hard on the eyes, which have trouble adjusting to the shifting light levels. You may find it uncomfortable, or possibly unsafe, if your eyes cannot recover quickly enough to recognize objects around you. If you have driven on a parkway on a sunny day in summer, where trees are planted along the side of the road, you may have experienced this strong contrast in light and dark.

Dark shade results where tree and shrubs are so dense or so close to the ground that almost all light is cut off. It is difficult to see color, and many plants struggle to grow under such conditions. Usually gardeners striving for flower color employ stopgap measures, such as planting small bulbs or annuals between the roots of a beech tree and replacing them every year. Another possibility is to remove some of the branches, so that flowering plants have enough light to grow.

Garden designers make good use of contrasting areas of light and shade. In a sunny, hot landscape, shade will be inviting and attractive. If the shade is light enough or if there is a transitional area in which color and objects can be discerned, the area will be even more attractive. In a cooler climate or a shady native garden, open areas where the sun can shine and different types of plants can grow can be just as appealing. In such a

case, the dimensions of the open area are important, since during different parts of the day and year, shade will occur in different parts of the open area; it is almost always necessary to observe the garden for a year to fine-tune the details. Future growth of the trees will need to be monitored for the same reason.

ARTIFICIAL LIGHT

Gardeners don't usually worry much about the effects of artificial lighting. The problem of metamerism, which describes a situation in which colors may match under one type of light but not under another, is a serious concern for many other artistic and design fields that produce or use textiles, paints, and dyes. Although gardeners rarely have a need to be concerned, it is worth noting that choosing or specifying colors for objects or plants that will be used in a garden should not be done under artificial lighting.

The two artificial-lighting situations that gardeners may be interested in are indoor lighting for flower shows and flower judging, and night illumination for gardens that are connected with living and entertaining spaces. Lighting engineers can deal with both situations, but here are some general guidelines on how color is affected.

Under incandescent light, which is the light used in most homes, things look yellowish. When professional photographers take pictures indoors, they use tungsten film, which corrects for this yellowish cast. Under incandescent light, reds and oranges look lighter and more saturated, blues and greens look darker and less saturated, and purples look more reddish. Under most fluorescent lighting available to homeowners, reds, oranges, and browns look darker and grayer, the value and saturation of blues and greens increases, and purples look more blue. There are also special fluorescent lights that can show colors as they appear in daylight; these are made specifically for color matching.

In residential outdoor lighting, the light color may range from warm to cool, but perhaps more important, night lighting for the home is of a lower intensity than average daylight, so it is more difficult to discriminate between colors. In both night lighting and indoor lighting for garden shows, the light is often more directional than diffused, that is, directed toward certain objects, such as a path or driveway outside, or certain parts of the displays indoors. If you look away from the light, where the shadows are, you find such a relatively small amount of light that it is often very difficult to make out any color. In this case, not only do you have the distortion from the color of the light, but the visible colors also change because of the relatively low level of light intensity. Good lighting is spread in such a way that the light and dark contrasts are not so great that they cause discomfort or leave areas too dark for safety.

The artificial lighting used at this indoor flower show is less intense and more directional than average daylight. The result is a scene with pools of yellowish light and undefined shadows.

The same green and white colors look quite different when seen
in a narrow, upright blade of ornamental grass and a broad,
floppy hydrangea plant.

TEXTURE

In botany, horticulture, and color science, texture is a critical element, and each of these fields uses specific terms for the various types of textures. In design, where such detailed classification is less of a constraint, several simple but broad designations suffice: surface and volume textures, smooth and rough surfaces, and fine and coarse volumes.

The concept of surface texture in horticulture relates to its use in textiles. Woven fabric can have a dimensional quality or a uniform, flat, or smooth aspect. This translates even more simply into rough or smooth; the terms are relative, not absolute, and describe a continuum. As an example found in the garden, leaves and flowers may be considered smooth in texture when compared to other objects such as tree bark, but not as smooth as a sheet of drawing paper or the interior walls of a house. The surfaces of the foliage of the oakleaf hydrangea and an ornamental grass will both appear to be smooth until you look closely. Then you find that the leaf of the hydrangea is less smooth, and this in turn affects the appearance of the surface color.

Volume texture in horticulture means the overall appearance of the plant, or in some cases, its leaves or flowers. It is generally described as fine or coarse. A plant's texture should be described in the context of a particular season or with reference to a particular part of the plant. Trees and woody plants often appear coarser or finer at different times of the year. In the study of color, volume color refers to translucency. It may be opaque (the ocean) or transparent (a soap bubble or glass). It is not related to the color descriptions that result from the concept of volume texture used in horticulture.

SURFACE TEXTURE—SMOOTH

The smoother a surface is, the greater its apparent saturation and light reflectance. When the color and intensity of the light change, a smooth surface gives a greater range of hue and value differences. You may already be aware of this relationship if you have examined glossy paint chips next to matte paint chips; because the glossy chips have a smoother surface, they can show a greater range of color, and their colors often appear more saturated.

A smooth surface reflects a greater amount of light in one direction, and if you are in a certain position, you will see on the surface a strong reflection that is the color of the light. This is called a highlight, or specular reflection. In the garden, the highlight will most often be white or light yellow in the middle of the day, but if the light is a different color, the highlight color will also change. Highlights can give depth to a picture or a garden scene, and they give us visual clues about distance. If the light is too strong, however, highlights can be annoying and even painful to the eyes and may distort accurate color discrimination. Because most gardens have a mixture of smooth and rough surfaces, such a problem is rarely a consideration in choosing plants. It may be more important when choosing hard surfaces such as garden furniture or paving to minimize distracting highlights.

Smoothness can increase to a glass-like state when rain or ice covers the surface of a plant with a smooth film. Not only are dirt and dust washed off, but the surface also appears more uniform. Every gardener knows that colors look richer and darker after a rain; these differences are actually measurable by visual comparison. Varnishes and other finishes have a similar effect on the colors of wood or painted or dyed surfaces. In the landscape, buildings and paved surfaces that have some sort of finish may be considered relatively smooth, and the colors will appear more saturated.

Direct light on a smooth-leaved hosta highlights a color sequence that ranges from whitish blue through green-yellow to blue-green, following the colors of the light and the shade.

Some textures that are rough on a larger scale can have an unexpected result when seen close up. Here, light catching the edges of fringed tulips creates highlights as great as a glossy surface would.

SURFACE TEXTURE—ROUGH

There are many types of rough surface textures in plant foliage and flowers. At the finest level, small hairs or other variations on the surface can be seen. At a more visible level, the margins of leaves or flowers may be wavy, cut, or fringed. The stems and bark of certain woody plants may be quite rough, such as the ridged surface of older oaks or the exfoliating bark of birches. Light reflects off a rough surface in many different directions, making direct color comparison with a color chip difficult, especially at close range. It is possible, however, to step back and compare colors at different distances if you are aware of the effects of optical mixing (see pp. 24-25).

As you consider these various textures of flowers, foliage, and hard surfaces, you begin to appreciate how important texture is in design composition. When an object can be viewed at varied distances, texture affects the interplay of depth and light, which in turn affects the apparent color of objects. Most plants in the garden are a combination of rough and smooth textures. For example, a hosta leaf may be smooth with ridged veins and wavy margins, and a tulip petal may be silky with fringed edges. As you step back from such plants, the tactile sensations decrease, and you are more likely to view the foliage or flower as being flat; you may have the feeling that you are looking at a photograph more than looking at an object in space.

Lamb's ears have such a rough surface that even rain can't make them smooth enough to have brilliant highlights. The water makes the plant look darker and more saturated (more green), but the range of colors is smaller because of the texture and the light.

Designers often employ rough surfaces to advantage in the garden. Where the glare of the sun is a problem, matte surfaces may minimize surface reflection. Because these surfaces appear less saturated, they can be used for plantings around building entrances or where signs, or directions, or works of art are to be the focus of attention. Rough surfaces make good backgrounds. Lawns (as opposed to individual blades of grass, which have a smooth surface) and mulch are rougher than most paved surfaces. Brick, stone, and concrete are smoother, but not as smooth as painted or finished surfaces. Rough in the garden often means more natural and less likely to compete for attention.

VOLUME TEXTURE—FINE

Plants are considered to be fine textured when their leaves, branches, or flowers are relatively small. Trees with needle leaves, such as conifers, flowers such as Queen Anne's lace, and foliage such as many of the grasses are just a few examples. As plants change their appearance during the seasons, their volume texture may shift. This is true of many trees; for example, honeylocust has a fine texture when it is in leaf and a medium texture in winter, when all you see are the branches. Plants may also shift when they are in flower; most daylilies, for example, have fine to medium foliage, but their flowers may be fine, medium, or coarse.

Fine-textured plants have parts of many colors, and each of these colors will absorb and reflect not only the light from the sun or sky, but also the light reflected from each of the other parts. This phenomenon adds depth and detail, increasing the feeling of complexity in a scene. So very often fine-textured plants are used to weave the colors of other plants into a composition by adding bits of colors that mix more readily than large areas of color.

Fine texture also affects color perception. The individual parts of a fine-textured plant are easily seen up close against a background of different color but start to mix optically with other fine-textured plants against a grayed background when the distance increases even by a couple of feet. When seen close up, the colors on a fine-textured plant may appear more different (simultaneous contrast), but when the

Queen Anne's lace is not often seen from a worm's-eye view, but it shows you some of the underlying colors that affect flower color in a normal view.

observer steps back, the colors may look more alike (color assimilation). Thus if you have plants that are complementary in color, they will begin to gray as the viewing distance increases instead of appearing as the bright or vivid opposites they seemed when seen at a close range. However, if you use colors that are close to each other on the color wheel (analogous colors), you will create a color that is the average of the two (or more) colors.

Other objects in the garden, including furniture or art, may function in the same way as fine-textured plants. The colors of delicate pieces of furniture or pieces of art may be seen clearly at a close distance, and blend in with adjoining colors when the viewing distance increases.

Volume Texture—Coarse

Although the word "coarse" has been used for some time to describe large leaves and flowers and large branches, the negative connotation of the word suggests that coarse-textured plants should not be used in gardens. However, if you remember that contrast is an important part of design, you will immediately realize how important it is to have coarse accents—foliage, flowers, furniture, or art—in your garden. It is necessary for visual relief as well as for a counterpoint to show off the fine textures of other plants. Coarse textures are also helpful if plants are to be seen from great distances and to show off great blocks of color.

The colors of coarse plants will not mix optically except at extreme distances, and so coarse plants are a good counterpoint to the fine- and medium-textured plants that may make up the garden. Even though they may not occupy the greatest area of color, they set the dominant color of a composition just by their large size. Knowing this may help you decide upon a particular color scheme for your flowers and foliage colors.

*The coarse foliage of castor bean and the flowers of the cannas provide
large areas of color. Even when seen from a distance, the blocks of color
stand out from the garden picture.*

TIME

Colors change with time. All artists learn that they must know their materials, such as pigments and dyes, canvas and paper, to predict how colors will fade or shift in hue as time passes. Garden designers, too, should consider time as a key element in garden design. It is often ignored but inexorably predictable in its effect on the life a flower, a leaf, the garden, and the larger landscape.

LIFE OF A FLOWER

Garden books often feature flowers at the peak of their bloom and full intensity of their color. These timeless flowers are perfect—no chewed edges, no mildew, no brown tips—as though the garden were part of a flower judging. It is interesting to think that modern horticulture takes a different view. Gardens are now thought to be healthier if they tolerate a certain level of pests and diseases. Perhaps garden design will also be healthier if it also tolerates a certain level of imperfection. If brown can be tolerated in our art and homes, it can also have a legitimate place in gardens.

Flowers do change in color as they begin and complete their blooming cycle, but not all flowers turn brown as they die. Some are a paler or more muted version of their bloom color. Hydrangeas turn beige with underlying colors, and hellebores turn lime green with underlying colors. A number of narcissus and tulips change color as they age. Most of the pink narcissus start out as light orange or orange, and the color fades to a paler hue; many of the white narcissus begin bloom as yellow, which fades to a pale yellow, and finally to white. Most popular flowering annuals keep their color reliably, although extremes in rain and heat may cause some colors to shift in hue as well as in saturation. Garden catalogs rarely describe these shifts because they are so subtle that many people don't notice them, and there has not generally been a demand for more specific information about the color of flowers. Accurate color description seems to be more of a concern among gardeners or designers who see a particular garden continuously or are trying to achieve a particular color or planting combination.

Autumn crocus gets paler as it progresses through its bloom cycle.

Many colors are seen in the foliage of coral bells: the veins, the underside, and the leaves at various stages of growth.

LIFE OF A LEAF

Like flowers, the leaves of ornamental woody and herbaceous plants have a tremendous range of color that changes during the life of the plant. New growth may be green-yellow to red-purple; veins may be lighter or darker, more yellowish green, or more bluish or reddish than the rest of the leaf. The color of the mature leaf is the one generally cited in descriptive horticultural texts, except when they describe noticeable shifts, such as the brilliant and breathtaking reds, yellows, and oranges of a New England autumn. There are also less spectacular color changes, as leaves turn various shades of browns and dull greens.

The leaves of most plants are lighter and less saturated on the underside, and this difference adds a sense of drama when light strikes the surface, when the wind blows and the leaves shift, or when you see through the leaf from the underside. For the most part, these color differences are quite small, so most people are not aware of the top and underside of a leaf as having separate colors. When the differences are greater, you may see it noted in the plant's name, such as silver maple, where the underside of the leaf is not only lighter, but actually shifts in hue from green-yellow toward green.

LIFE OF A GARDEN

A garden has a life cycle, and its early and late periods during the year can be as beautiful as its peak bloom time. If you look at the garden carefully when you are not distracted by the saturated colors of flowers, you should be able to think about the colors that form the structure of your garden. The woody landscape plants have bark, limbs, and stems that all have different colors of browns and greens. Wherever you live, you will have soil, sand, or stone, as well as grasses or plants that stay green year-round. When you look out on the landscape, you may initially just see grays, browns, and greens, but if you examine the colors more carefully, placing them next to each other or next to color chips of known color, you can discern the subtle differentiation in hue, value, and saturation. This sort of analysis will prepare you to select flowers and foliage for the rest of the year. It will also give you a great appreciation of the colors found in nature.

When you know the underlying colors of your garden, you can plan for its decorative color. One of the challenges facing gardeners is to anticipate color cycles so the garden can have colors that work well together at various times. In display gardens, pots may be sunk into the ground to fill in spaces in which there is "no color," or other means may be used to ensure continuous bloom or interesting foliage. For home gardeners not interested in going to such extremes, considering local colors helps build a coherent garden color scheme.

In a well-designed mixed border, color changes mark the passage of summer months.

The flower colors of a perennial garden are seen against the colors of the summer landscape beyond.

Seen just at the cusp of fall, a mixture of saturated flower colors and the muted colors of grasses and sedums announce the change of seasons.

PASSAGE OF SEASONS

Seasonal color in plants can be outdoors or indoors and either separated from or joined with the local landscape. Outdoors, the colors are more often dictated by local conditions, even though the garden may be a collection of plants from other parts of the country or world. For example, in the mid-Atlantic region, the colors of the trees and shrubs are green-yellow in spring, green in summer, red to yellow in fall, and brown in winter; the light varies as the sun is higher in the sky in the summer, lower in fall and spring, and lowest in winter. The local colors for any area of the world can be described by season if you know the predominant local plants, the light conditions, and the prevailing weather patterns.

Some display gardens that are designed for maximum color impact are changed with the seasons and may be designed to harmonize with a particular building or interior feature. Seasonal color in this sense has a somewhat different meaning, although its roots are drawn from the colors we associate with the changing of the landscape. Such seasonal color is a large part of the business of horticulture. In the past, seasonal plants from wholesale growers were limited not only in color, but also in species. As a result, some attractive and reliable flowering plants are now in disfavor because of overuse. It is worthwhile noting that colors that are seen over and over may give a sense of comfort, but may also be ignored or actively disliked. This design problem is solved when growers and designers offer a wider selection of flowering plants or choose cultivars that offer different colors, or when the designer knows how to alter the appearance of certain colors.

Indoors, gardeners can grow and force plants from all over the world to bloom and display color during all seasons. Growers often concentrate on flowers for various seasonal events. Thus we tend to think of seasonal colors as display colors—yellow for daffodils in the spring, reds and yellows for the more common blooming annuals such as geraniums and marigolds in summer, the reds, oranges and yellows that are found in chrysanthemums for fall, and the red of poinsettias for winter. In recent years, the selection, and therefore the color range, of the seasonal colors has grown, but the basic colors still dominate. The marketing of new seasonal colors and species has been most successful when they are variations of the basic colors, such as daffodils that are bicolored or geraniums that are pink or peach, or when a plant that is well known, such as the poinsettia, is introduced in a range of different colors.

Passage of Years

The longer-lived members of the garden mark the passage of time most noticeably as they grow in size and affect the scale and organization of the garden. Their size also changes the blocks of color that are seen and the colors that are reflected back in the garden. Trees and large shrubs have the greatest effect; gardeners in new homes with bare lots bemoan the lack of mature trees more than other features. Since many large trees and shrubs in the garden grow so slowly, the effect of their growth on the color in the garden is sometimes ignored. Overgrown trees and shrubs can throw the colors out of balance and can block light needed in the garden not only for plant growth and bloom but also for adequate color vision.

When large trees and shrubs succumb to disease or severe weather, the mature garden looks strikingly different. The foliage colors and their reflected light colors are missing from the composition, and the amount of light that reaches the garden can change drastically. Areas that were formerly dark and shaded areas can become open, sunny patches of light.

Parts of the Haupt Garden at the Smithsonian Institution in Washington, D.C., were designed around a large European linden tree that was already growing there. Unfortunately, the tree died and had to be removed. In its place, a different type of planting creates a very different effect.

The intricate and beautiful detail of many plants is best viewed close
up. Stepping back changes the visual field. Some of the individual
details are lost, but you see a composition of flower and foliage color.

VISUAL FIELD

What a person sees in one look, without consciously moving the eyes, is considered to be the visual field. Every time you shift your glance or move through a garden, you are changing the visual field, which makes the concept more comprehensive than if you think like a painter or photographer, for whom the edge of the visual field is defined by the edge of the canvas or what is seen through the view finder of a camera. If you are standing next to another person and each of you is looking at the same object, each person's visual field will differ slightly, but not significantly. The two of you can discuss a certain view or part of the garden and understand each other perfectly. The idea of visual field makes the challenge that faces garden designers who are trying to compose a garden picture more similar to photography than it is to painting. Unlike the painter, who begins the process with a blank canvas and adds objects and colors until it conveys the desired scene, the garden designer (and the photographer) is faced with a jumble of plants,

structures, long and short views, and variable lighting and weather, and must remove or move objects, changing and restricting other views to create the desired scene. The restriction and controlling of views has always been a great part of garden design and directly affects the ways in which color is seen.

A SINGLE PLANT OR FLOWER

In order to design with visual field in mind, you must begin at the basic level of a single plant or flower. To know how to place any single plant in your garden, you must be able to define its characteristics. Horticulturists have keying systems to identify a plant and tell you if the plant will do well in a certain location. Designers can describe a plant in terms of form or shape, size, texture, and color, and then consider the site, calling it background or context, studying views, light, texture and color. This is the way a designer decides if a plant will look good in a certain location.

If you are looking to place an individual plant to show its color to advantage, you should now know enough to do so. You can describe the hue, value, and saturation of the various parts of the plant, and you can describe how those colors are modified by size, texture, lighting, and distance of viewing, so you can estimate how the colors will separate or mix together. Although such attention to individual plants is more the realm of the botanist or horticulturist than it is of the designer, it is where you develop your knowledge of plant color. You can probably design a large border or planting without focusing on too many of the details of individual plants, but if you are dissatisfied when looking at your planting, you will find this process of examining colors useful. It is why many garden designers are themselves gardeners; the best way to see individual flower and foliage colors as they change through the day and year is by working in the garden every day.

As you go through the steps of identification, you will find that they become almost intuitive, and you will be able to predict where plants will be displayed to their greatest advantage. The relationships that you discover in one plant will always have some application when deciding where to put other plants, so you will be building for yourself a mental and visual library of colors that work well together.

PLANT COMBINATIONS

The next step after learning about the color of one plant is to start pairing plants in different color combinations. This is one of the most enjoyable parts of garden design, because a relatively small change in a companion planting (as opposed to altering the entire background) can also change a garden composition. Some groupings are pleasing to so many people that you see them used (or perhaps overused) everywhere.

Many public gardens have color displays where the flowering and foliage plants are planted in drifts of color, so that they touch more than one other plant. If you visit these gardens or plant such a trial bed for yourself, you can study closely the effect of various colors on an individual plant. You can also estimate the effect of changing the amounts (more or less) or placement (front to back of the bed or side to side) upon the way the colors are seen. A mass of yellow flowers in front of a mass of dark red flowers will have a completely different effect visually than if the dark red flowers are place in front. You can also practice color combinations in a smaller way at a plant nursery; choose a plant you're interested in using in your garden and carry it through the nursery, seeing how it looks in front of various flowering and woody plants.

Many gardening books and magazines show plant combinations in close-up photos where the surrounding garden is not visible. This eliminates the effect of the other colors, which is particularly useful to beginning designers who are trying to decide how to combine plants and who would find a large garden or

Look closely at this garden scene, and note the light and dark colors and the
colors of greater or less saturation, as well as the hues. You should be able to see
colors blending and separating as you focus on different sections of this
complex planting scheme.

planting confusing. Breaking the design into smaller vignettes is a way of making the design problem approachable. It is also useful because these plant combinations can be used together not only as part of a complicated border, but also as the focus of attention in a smaller, less complicated design, such as the front of a house, around a mailbox, alongside a driveway, or any other setting where the combination might work to advantage.

If, at some point, the combination is to be part of a larger complicated planting, the transition between your plant combination and other plantings becomes critical. You will need to ensure that the separate scenes are joined seamlessly or separated so that they influence each other less.

GARDEN ROOM

The traditional way in which garden designers have separated scenes and colors is the creation of garden rooms, an organizing device in which the garden is separated into parts, much as a house is separated into rooms. The purpose may be functional (such as separating the patio and its summer border from the vegetable garden and the compost pile), or the separation may be aesthetic, in which case you may have a red garden separate from a white garden or a spring garden separate from a summer border. In each case, an organizational tool helps you control the visual field. The jumble of colors, shapes, and sizes can be controlled and made to convey your ideas and focus attention on certain parts of the garden.

You can begin to think of this visual organization as you look out on your garden from rooms in your house; the views that you see are restricted by the limits of the window frame, and the colors depend upon the objects and the light. Generally, it is darker inside your home than it is outside, so during much of the day, the garden will appear lighter. The background of your garden may be seen differently from different windows; on the first floor, you are more likely to have the color of the sky as part of the background, on higher floors, you are more likely to see soil, grass, and green undergrowth as the background of the garden. The distance from the garden will determine whether or not you see the flowers and foliage as separate plants

Dividing the garden into "rooms" is a traditional way to control the visual field. At top, a fence and arch frame a partial view into the garden. In the photo above, the hedge both restricts the view of the landscape and acts as a background for the mixed planting.

*The dark green arched hedge frames the initial view into this
multicolored garden, setting the scene for a dramatic entry.*

or whether they have begun to mix optically; probably most of the small detail will have already mixed in with the plant color as a whole.

As you move into your garden, the colors you see will be affected at first by where you have been. If you've come from inside the house, you will have to adjust to the change in lightness; if you've come from another part of the garden that was more green, or orange or any other color, you will have to adjust to the effects of successive contrast (see p. 101). If there is an entryway, such as a brick or stone gate or a green trellis or hedge, the colors you see will be framed by these colors; if the light conditions are different, the garden will appear lighter or darker. If the view of the garden is partially blocked, as by the overhang of a tree or a trellised vine, the composition of the colors will change as you enter the garden. Walls and hedges may partly or entirely block views of colors within parts of the garden and views of the landscape beyond. The colors beyond may be more natural, as a woodlands or desert, or may be a mixture of housing and foliage at near and far distances. The more complex the background, the more difficult to predict how color combinations in your garden will appear.

As you move through the garden, the light will change with your direction of viewing; you may experience strong direct lighting or diffused lighting, which will affect the saturation and value contrasts around you. As you move, the placement of the colors will change in the visual field; colors that are side by side may change to front to back, other colors may enter the field, and the relative amounts of each color will shift as you move. As you prepare to leave the garden, the colors you have just seen will influence the next views you see.

Perhaps your garden may be seen from the street or from other gardens. The colors that you see inside the garden are influenced by the new surroundings outside the garden as well. Again, frame, lighting, and distance changes will affect how you see the colors that are viewed.

COMPOSING WITH COLOR

*A*s a way of organizing your thoughts about color design in a garden, start by imagining the color sequences that will exist. Think first of the background colors and light; think of the colors of the soil and more long-lived trees and shrubs. Look at the way the light changes as the seasons and weather change, and as the light is reflected from and passes through all the vegetation around you. Then plan the ways in which people will come to view your garden. Imagine how they will see different parts of your garden and in what sequence. Decide if they will need to be closer to see all the garden colors, or farther away. Look at how the background colors will change, and decide if they need to be partially or entirely blocked with other background colors. Start composing with plants you know and add color variations with different combinations of plants and furnishings. The garden will constantly change, but with the basic knowledge of how color behaves, you can accommodate and enhance the changes, building a beautiful work of art.

In this display, drifts of separated plantings are orchestrated to form cascading blocks of color.

COLOR DISPLAYS

Color displays come in all sizes, shapes, and colors, but they all have the same purpose: to look good and to appeal to non-gardeners as well as gardeners. There are great formal display gardens, where flowers are arranged in geometric patterns with blocks of color or in drifts of color in borders. Smaller display gardens may be in front of homes, offices, stores, or at the entryways to parks and towns. Even smaller bursts of color may be found in planters, containers, and window boxes. Color displays may also be roadside plantings of bulbs or perennials, or specimen plantings of flowering trees such as cherry blossoms or crepe myrtles.

The key to all display plantings is the ability to attract attention, so saturated colors play an important part in the design. Colors may be massed for spectacular impact or blended for more subtle effects. Color combinations may be relatively static, such as summer plantings of bedding plants that stay the same for several months, or they may appear to change in a more rapid succession, mimicking the natural cycles of blooming, such as spring-flowering bulbs when combined with and followed by the emerging growth of spring- and summer-flowering perennials.

Arranging color displays for maximum impact means paying careful attention to viewpoints. Consider if the angle of viewing will be from one or many sides, if it will be from above or below the planting, if it will be from a distance or nearby, and think about what the background colors will be. From a color-blending point of view, the distance, angle of viewing, and background will determine how the color display stands out from its surroundings. If the surroundings (whether they are buildings, trees, or other plantings) are too confusing or difficult to work with, they may be blocked partially or fully in the display design. If you can make the planting work with the surroundings, you'll create a display garden that can be copied but not duplicated, due to the unique combination of local light and color background.

Displays may be open to the public only during certain daylight hours, or the display may be always available for viewing. Colors that are seen more clearly in different intensities of light may be blended into a single composition, or separated so that certain parts of the display are more prominent at different times of day. Many plants used for display purposes can tolerate a wide range of cultural conditions, so that within a broad range, the designer can alter the site to create a particular effect, allowing the combination of plants that might not naturally occur together.

Display gardens are also designed for specialized purposes or particular populations, such as hospitals, nursing homes, and schools. When designing such a planting, you must consider the limitations or preferences for color viewing among these populations—their age, health, and attitudes—as well as traditional design considerations.

In New York City's Central Park, the formal flower displays change color regularly to reflect the season.

*A native garden in the Midwest. Recognized plantings echo the
local colors, imparting a feeling of comfort.*

Native Gardens

Native gardens or naturalized plantings often have as their basic design challenge the problem of creating a garden from what is normally considered background planting. The key is drawing attention to plants and plant combinations that are usually considered a backdrop for other types of gardens. The colors may be more subdued than those found in display plantings, and they are the colors that are seen everywhere in the local area, and so are taken for granted or ignored. In addition, native gardens have, by definition, a more restricted universe of plants and planting sites from which the designer can draw. Sometimes this universe is expanded when plants that have been introduced to the native habitat are considered naturalized and acceptable for the purposes of the individual garden, but the palette is still relatively limited.

In native gardens, perhaps more than any other type of gardening, the site drives the design. The growing conditions may be critical to where certain plants can be grown, so that the designer, instead of adapting the site to fit a design idea, is more likely to adapt the design idea to fit the site. Some growing conditions are closely linked to the design considerations, such as light. Certain plant populations may exist only under certain types of lighting—light shade or open sun. This, then, may restrict the play of light and shade, which can be a great part of garden design.

To make garden visitors aware of the unique colors of a native garden, sometimes it is necessary merely to exaggerate color groupings that occur in nature so that they are more visible. A massed group of a common native looks entirely different than individual specimens scattered throughout the landscape. The rhythm and repetition of natural color sequences can be enlarged or magnified to make these patterns more noticeable. If space doesn't permit such expansion, look for settings and backgrounds that will alter the color appearance of certain plants; focus your attention on certain parts of the garden.

Walls and hedges can block and control views for the homeowner faced with confusing background colors.

RESIDENTIAL GARDENS

Unlike the native garden, which is restricted to the colors found in the local environment, residential gardens often are surrounded by an unlimited number of colors, sometimes having nothing to do with the local environment. Within view of many homes is not only a variety of landscaping colors, resulting from a mix of plants, but also a variety of manmade colors, from house and trim to walls, fences, paving, art, and furniture colors. These varied colors form the background colors for anything the home gardener creates, and in most cases, it is not possible to block off these colors completely. Most people aren't really aware of this as a design problem, and don't realize that if their gardens don't look quite as they imagined, that this multicolored background may be at fault.

Home gardeners generally have a choice of views with one of two backgrounds. They look at their garden (or gardens) from the house or porch, patio, or deck, and either walls, hedges or other homes and landscaping are the backdrop for their view. Or they look at the house, which becomes the background for gardens in front of or slightly to the side of the house. The distances involved in these views determine what will be seen clearly and what colors will start to blend.

When you look at the garden from outside the house, you'll see the colors that are next to or near the house. If next to or surrounded by the house, they will be subject to simultaneous contrast (see pp. 94-101). Some houses have colors that are more difficult to work with or that don't work well with the intended garden colors. In most cases, separating the dissonant colors with hedging or foliage framework (usually thought of as foundation plantings) is the simplest and most traditional way of solving the problem.

When you look at the garden from inside the house, you'll see the garden colors in front of fences and hedges, if the yard is enclosed, or in front of other homes and their landscaping. If the colors in your garden don't seem to look the way you want them to, it may be that you will need to provide a more appropriate background. Hedges and walls can be of a single color or of related colors, and in many cases can block outside views almost completely, giving more control over the garden picture.

A question always arises as to what colors go well with each other or with the house. These are personal decisions, and the clues to making these decisions can come from color combinations you like in other situations—fashion, home interiors, graphics—or simply a group of colors that you notice and enjoy. However, keep in mind that the background colors in nature are darker and grayer than graphic and fashion colors, and so any saturated colors will look even brighter and lighter than they may appear alone.

Anyone who gardens is, at a practical level, a color designer. When you move a plant, place a path, or select a piece of garden furniture, you are designing with color. Having read about and seen visual examples of a systematic way to think and communicate about color, you are now more aware of all the colors around you. If you have found this approach useful, you will be enthusiastic about further study and observation.

Of course, the simplest way to move beyond this book is just to sit and watch. Mimic the artists who observe the same scene at different times of day and during different seasons. Notice how the color combinations of flowers and foliage in your garden change during the active gardening year. Keep notes of what you like, or sketch or take photographs of colors that you find interesting. If you want to develop your sense of color relationships, you will need a color system—color chips that you can use as a reliable standard and to sensitize your eye to detail. As you become increasingly aware of the small details of color, you will develop an acute awareness of all the colors in your garden. Not only will the striking combinations of orange and purple flowers rivet your attention, but also the more subtle combinations—the reflected colors in water, the colors of trees, and the colors of the sky. The common colors around us set the scene for all garden design.

FURTHER READING

Albers, J. *Interaction of Color.* rev. 1987. New Haven, Conn.: Yale University Press, 1975. A short version of this important artist's work.

Chevreul, M. E. *Principles of Harmony and Contrast of Colors and Their Application to the Arts.* rev. ed. by Faber Birren. West Chester, Pa.: Schiffer Publishing, 1987. A classic work, often cited by artists.

Evans, R.M. *An Introduction to Color.* rep. 1965. New York: John Wiley & Sons, 1948. An excellent reference about observed color, now out of print; includes some math.

Gerritsen, F. *Theory and Practice of Color.* New York: Van Nostrand Reinhold, 1983. A visual study, out of print, worth looking for in the library.

Luke, J. T. *The Munsell Color System: A Language for Color.* New York: Fairchild Publications, 1996. A reference for artists and designers that includes the Munsell Student Set (200 color chips) for observations.

Hobhouse, P. *Color in Your Garden.* rev. ed. New York: Little, Brown and Co., 1985. Good observations in this popular gardening book slanted toward the plants and tastes of England.

Huse, R. D. and K.L. Kelly. *A Contribution Toward Standardization of Color Names in Horticulture.* The American Rhododendron Society, 1984. A precise numeric comparison of RHS and Munsell color charts.

Jekyll, G. *Colour Schemes for the Flower Garden,* rev. ed. Salem, N.H.: The Ayer Company, 1983. The classic. Always worth rereading; like the Hobhouse book, English in its approach.

Jones, L. A., et al. Committee on Colorimetry, *The Science of Color.* Washington, D.C.: Optical Society of America, 1963, reissue 1973. Periodically revised, this technical compendium is a good source for information on a wide range of color topics.

Rossotti, H. *Colour/Why the World Isn't Grey.* Princeton, N.J.: Princeton University Press, 1989. The science of color, written for the general reader.

Swirnoff, L. *Dimensional Color.* Boston: Birkhauser, 1989. Out of print, but useful for landscape architects.

Verity, E. *Color Observed.* rev. pocket ed., New York: Van Nostrand Reinhold, 1980. Out of print; mostly text, but written for artists; informative reading.

Zelanski, P. and M.P. Fischer. *Color.* 2nd ed., Englewood Cliffs, N.J.: Prentice-Hall, 1994. A useful popular book, aimed toward graphic artists.

SELECTED REFERENCES

Color Aid Corporation, 37 East 18th St., New York, NY 10003. This company produces high-quality colored papers useful for teaching and constructing models.

Color Marketing Group, 5904 Richmond Highway, Suite 408, Alexandria, VA 22303. An international not-for-profit group of color designers for many industries.

Inter-Society Color Council, 11491 Sunset Hills Rd., Suite 301, Reston, VA 22090. A technical society for color professionals.

Munsell Book of Color. Macbeth, 405 Little Britain Road, New Windsor, NY 12553-6148. This is the complete set of 1,600 color chips; not very portable for gardeners but an excellent reference.

Royal Horticultural Society Colour Chart. RHS Enterprises Limited, The Royal Horticultural Society's Garden, Wisley, Woking, Surrey GU23 6PB England. Color fans including 800 color swatches; more portable than the Munsell book, but difficult to separate into regular steps of hue, value, and saturation.

PHOTO CREDITS

INDEX

BOOK PUBLISHER: *Jim Childs*

ASSOCIATE PUBLISHER: *Helen Albert*

EDITORIAL ASSISTANT: *Cherilyn DeVries*

DESIGNER/LAYOUT ARTIST: *Henry Roth*

EDITOR: *Ruth Dobsevage*

TYPEFACE: *ITC Legacy*

PAPER: *Warren Patina Matte, 70-lb., neutral pH*

PRINTER: *R. R. Donnelley, Willard, Ohio*